Things To Do in Children's Worship Book 3

by Susan Sayers

Kevin
Mayhew

First published in 1999 by
KEVIN MAYHEW LTD
Buxhall
Stowmarket
Suffolk IP14 3DJ

Things To Do in Children's Worship, Book 3, is adapted from *Living Stones*
by Susan Sayers, published by Kevin Mayhew, 1997, 1998.

0 1 2 3 4 5 6 7 8 9

ISBN 1 84003 332 0
Catalogue No 1500252

Cover design by Sara Walker
Edited by Peter Dainty
Typesetting by Richard Weaver
Printed in Great Britain

Foreword

In this book, I hope to provide material for use in children's worship which is helpful to those churches which do not follow a set programme of readings and themes. The material is arranged thematically, first in broad categories and then, by way of the indices at the back of the book, in a more detailed manner. When planning for children's work, it is advisable to read through the suggested Bible passages prayerfully. You are then in a better position to see how the programme relates to the theme, and also to supplement and vary the material as a result of your own insights and the specific needs of your group.

A few general ideas about storytelling:

- Tell the story from the viewpoint of the character in the situation. To create the time-machine effect, avoid eye contact as you slowly put on the appropriate cloth or cloak, and then make eye contact as you meet the children in character.

- Have an object with you which leads into the story – a water jug or lunch box, for instance.

- Walk the whole group through the story, so that they are physically moving from one place to another; and use all kinds of places, such as broom cupboards, under the stairs, outside under the trees, and so on. Needless to say, every care should be taken to ensure children's safety wherever you work with them.

- Collect some carpet tiles – blue and green – so that at story time the children can sit around the edge of these and help you position the cut-outs for the story.

May God bless you all, and the children with whom you worship.

SUSAN SAYERS

Contents

THE STORY OF JESUS
Saying 'Yes' to God   8
The Wise Men   9
Escaping to Egypt   10
The Childhood of Jesus   11
Jesus is Baptised   12
Jesus Meets His Disciples   13
Jesus' Temptations   14
Water into Wine   15
Jesus Calls Peter   16
The Twelve Disciples   17
Saying Thank You   18
Jesus Stills the Storm   19
Walking on Water   20
Who Is Jesus?   21
Jesus on the Mountain   22
Jesus and Zacchaeus   23
Jesus Is Anointed   24
Palm Sunday   25
Jesus Our King   26
Easter Day   27
The Road to Emmaus   28
Seeing and Believing   30
Peter Starts Again   32
Jesus Goes to Heaven   33
Jesus the Word of God   34

PARABLES
Salt and Light   36
The Seed of God's Word   37
The Costly Pearl   38
The Wise and Foolish Bridesmaids   39
The Talents   40
Real Wealth   41
Following Instructions   42
Lost and Found   43
Forgiveness   44
The Rich Man and Lazarus   46

FOLLOWING JESUS
The Good Shepherd   48
Jesus the Way   49
Counting the Cost   50

Obeying Jesus   51
The Proof of Obedience   52
Carrying Our Cross   53
The Easy Yoke   54
Friends of Jesus   55
Faithful Service   56

THE GOOD LIFE
Choosing God's Way   58
As Loving as God   59
Loving Our Enemies   60
Putting Others First   61
Words and Deeds   62
Flourishing and Fruitful   63
Slave or Free?   64
God's or Caesar's?   65
Thirsting for God   66
Moving On   67
Imagining Heaven   68

PROPHETS
Elijah and the Prophets of Baal   70
Elijah and Naboth's Vineyard   71
Isaiah and Jesus   72
Amos and the Plumb Line   73
John the Baptist   74

PRAYER
Stop and Listen   76
Persistent Prayer   77
Acceptable Prayer   78
The Lord's Prayer   79
Wants and Needs   80

THE CHURCH AND ITS MISSION
Pentecost   82
The Body of Christ   83
Spreading the Message   84
Good News for All Nations   85
Guided by God's Spirit   86

MISCELLANEOUS
God's Creation   88
The Holy Trinity   89
A Holy Day   90

INDEX OF USES   91

THE STORY OF JESUS

Saying 'Yes' to God

Things to read

Hebrews 10:5-10
Luke 1:26-56

Things to do

Aim: To explore what it meant for Mary to say 'Yes'.

Have a team game which needs team members to co-operate (football is the obvious choice, or you could try French cricket or pass the balloon between the knees).

Find out if anyone has ever been asked to play for the school team or orchestra, or sing in the choir. Have some pictures of well-known footballers and actors as well. Talk about how pleased and proud you feel to be asked to do an important job, but bring out the point that you can't just go along to play in the match or act in the performance. What other things would you have to do? List both the up- and the down-sides of such a privilege. Looking at it as a whole, would they still want to take it on? (You could vote on it.)

Have another sheet with a picture of Mary in the middle. It is headed, 'Chosen to be Jesus' mother'.

Look at what Mary was chosen for, and on one side of the picture list all the good things about it. Then think over Jesus' life and see if you can think of any sad, painful or difficult things that might be part of the job. List these on the other side of the picture. How would they feel about taking on the job?

At the bottom write, 'Mary still said "Yes!".' It amazed her that God had chosen her, and it made her realise how wonderful and sensible and patient and courageous God was to set about saving the world in this way.

Mary went to visit her cousin Elizabeth, who was six months pregnant with John the Baptist at the time, and both Mary and Elizabeth (and John) were filled with excitement and delight at what God was up to.

Things to pray

My soul glorifies the Lord
and my spirit rejoices in God my saviour.

Have some happy music on to dance to and while the music is still playing everyone claps a rhythm and shouts to it.

The Wise Men

Things to read

Isaiah 60:1-6
Matthew 2:1-12

Things to do

Aim: To explore why the wise men made their journey and what they found out.

Who am I? Fix a picture of an animal or food item on everyone's back. They have to find out who they are by going round asking questions about themselves. The others can only answer yes or no.

Point out how in the game they had to search for the right answer, and it was like a journey to find the truth. Today we are looking at some wise men who set out on a similar quest.

Have three adults meeting up as if they are the wise men resting on the journey and chatting together about what the day has been like, what they miss, and what they are hoping to find. (It is best to try out the conversation beforehand.)

When the wise men have settled down for the night (or gone to feed the camels), show the children a sheet of paper with these headings on it: Who? What? Why? In the different sections brainstorm ideas about who they were (wise men from the East), what they were doing (following a star to find a baby king of great importance) and why they bothered (they had worked out from the signs that this birth was really important, and they wanted to be there to pay their respects). Use the children's words, of course.

Now have the wise men on their way back, talking about how they felt about King Herod, what it was like to see Jesus, and why they are going home by a different route.

Next you will need lots of lining paper or rolls of wallpaper. The best present we can give to Jesus is ourselves. Working in twos, the children draw round each other on the paper, cut themselves out and colour them. On the front write:

Jesus, the best present I can give you is myself!

Things to pray

Have some incense, gold and myrrh on display during the teaching. As each is brought to the front pray together:

Gold
The wise men brought gold to Jesus.
Jesus, we bring you the gold of our
    obedience.
Help us to live as you want us to.
Amen.

Frankincense
The wise men brought frankincense.
Jesus, we bring you the incense of our
    worship.
You are God and we worship you.
Amen.

Myrrh
The wise men brought myrrh.
Jesus, we bring you the myrrh of the
    world's sadness.
Help us to look after one another better.
Amen.

Escaping to Egypt

Things to read
Psalm 31:1-8
Matthew 2:13-23

Things to do

Aim: To get to know the events of Matthew's account of Jesus' birth and the escape into Egypt.

Shh! Sit in a circle with one person blindfolded in the centre. Someone starts to walk around the circle carrying something noisy, such as a bunch of keys. The person in the centre tries to hear where they are. If they point to the right place, they get to carry the keys and someone else is blindfolded.

Tell the escape story from the Gospel reading with everyone making the sound effects and miming the actions. Everyone lies asleep, wakes up, yawns, listens, packs secretly, opens and closes the door very carefully, walks through the town without making any noise at all, looks around whenever there's a noise in case it's Herod, and shouts 'Yes!' when they eventually reach Egypt. Show them on a map where Bethlehem is in relation to Egypt, and then trace the return journey, reading from Matthew the reason given for not returning to Bethlehem.

Things to pray
Lord, keep us safe
as we travel through life.
Help us to love what is good
and hate what is evil. Amen.

The Childhood of Jesus

Things to read

1 Samuel 2:18-20, 26
Luke 2:41-52

Things to do

Aim: To understand that Jesus shared a human childhood, and to look at the kind of experiences he would probably have had.

Sit in a circle and pass round a toy as each person has a turn to speak. Only the one holding the toy can speak. The first round is 'What I liked best about this Christmas was . . .' Anyone not wanting to speak just passes the toy on. The next round is 'The job I hate having to do is . . .'

Have a timeline displayed to help the children place Jesus' birth in its historical context from Abraham to the present day. Have available some library books, travel brochures and Bibles with pictures of Palestine under the Romans and some photographs of the country surrounding Bethlehem. Have a large flat stone or board to demonstrate grinding flour and kneading dough, and a display of some of the raisins and dates and nuts that would have been grown and eaten.

Give the children a 'living museum' experience of what life would have been like for Jesus and his friends, bringing in whatever examples and artefacts you can get hold of. You may for instance be able to borrow some fabric or traditional clothing from the area, or traditional lamps or bedrolls, or you could use the pictures. The more involved the children are the better.

They can find out about sitting cross-legged on the floor and chanting from memory in school, and the kind of local jobs that would be the equivalent of a paper round, such as sheep watching, or helping with the harvest.

Things to pray

Jesus, you know what it's like
to be the same age as me.
Remind me that I can
talk things over with you
whenever I want
and you always
have time to listen. Amen.

Jesus is Baptised

Things to read
Isaiah 42:1-9
Matthew 3:13-17

Things to do
Aim: To get to know Matthew's account of Jesus' baptism.

Have a look at some atlases, picture books and travel brochures to find out where the River Jordan is and what it looks like.

Wrap a 'camel hair shirt' round some-one and stand him in the River Jordan (barefoot on a blue sheet). Can they guess who this is? If not, introduce them to John the Baptist. Remind them that John is using the water as a sign of the people drowning to their old sinful lives and coming up with their sins forgiven by God, so they are clean and ready for when the Messiah comes. The Messiah, or Christ, is God's anointed one who will come and save his people.

Today we hear what happened when Jesus himself came to the River Jordan. He was about thirty years old at the time. (Have someone to be Jesus, walking into the river.) He asks John to baptise him, but John feels it ought to be the other way round. (Why?)

But Jesus persuades him that it is right for him to be baptised with every-one else, so John does it. (They act this out.) As soon as Jesus has been baptised, it's as if the heavens open up, and God's Spirit comes down to rest on him. It looks like a dove flying down to him. And there is a voice from heaven which says, 'This is my Son, whom I love; I am well pleased with him!' Have the words displayed so that everyone can say them together.

Things to pray
Jesus, I believe and trust
that you are God's Son,
the promised Saviour,
the Christ, the Messiah of God. Amen.

Jesus Meets His Disciples

Things to read

Isaiah 49:1-7
John 1:35-51

Things to do

Aim: To get to know John's account of the disciples meeting Jesus and deciding to follow him.

Divide the children into pairs, giving each pair one half of an old Christmas card. One of the pair goes looking for the hidden piece of the picture and when they have seen it, they leave it where it is and go and sit down at one end of the room, saying nothing. Meanwhile the others are sitting at the other end of the room, following their partner with their eyes. At a given signal, once everyone is back, the group with one half of the picture go to the hidden part, collect it and join their partner. The first pair with the completed picture wins.

Talk about how their partners had shown them exactly where to find what they wanted, so they were able to go straight to it, without wasting any time. Today we are going to find out how some people were helped by their friends to find someone they were looking for.

Using the carpet tiles method, let the children help to build up a picture of a road, some houses and trees (palm and sycamore), lake and distant hills. We are in Galilee about two thousand years ago. Go through the account in John's Gospel, with cut-out pictures of John the Baptist, Jesus, Andrew and his unnamed friend, Simon Peter, Philip and Nathanael. You can base these on the pictures below. (Beforehand practise talking through the events and moving the characters around with John's Gospel beside you as your 'script'.)

Talk with the children about the way we always want our friends to share any good news, and that's what happened here.

Things to pray

Jesus, I want my friend . . .
to meet you and find out how good it is to live in your company. Amen.

Jesus' Temptations

Things to read

Genesis 2:15-17; 3:1-7
Matthew 4:1-11

Things to do

Aim: To know about Jesus' temptations in the desert.

Prepare some coloured pieces of paper and some white pieces with questions on. Stick them on to people with sticky tape. The questions have to team up with the right answers. Here are some suggestions:

What colour is a banana?	Blue
What colour is grass?	Yellow
What colour is the sky?	Black
What colour is coal?	Green

Borrow some library books to show the children some pictures of the desert where Jesus went to be on his own with God after he had been baptised. Use a yellow or brown and a blue towel laid on the floor as the background to the story, and sit the children round the edge. Explain that to fast means to go without food, and people sometimes do this when they are praying, especially if they are wanting to find out God's will for them in their life.

After he had been baptised, Jesus went off into the desert to fast and pray. He wanted to make sure he was really listening to God as he didn't want to get it wrong. As you tell the story of the three temptations, place the following objects on the background:

1. A loaf of bread (stone shaped) and a large stone. (Satan was homing in on Jesus' feeling hungry: personal comfort and survival.)

2. A high tower built of bricks and a cut-out question mark. (Satan was picking up on Jesus wondering who he was and what his job would be exactly.)

3. A wrapped present and a bill or invoice. (Satan suggested a way for Jesus to give his Father a present – but it came with a crazy price tag.)

As you tell the story, place beside each set of objects the answers Jesus used:

1. Matthew 4, verse 4
2. Matthew 4, verse 7
3. Matthew 4, verse 10

Things to pray

Lord Jesus,
when I am tempted to do what is wrong
and unloving and selfish,
make me brave
and keep me strong. Amen.

Water into Wine

Things to read

Psalm 36:5-10
John 2:1-11

Things to do

Aim: To see the wedding at Cana as a sign of God's glory shown in Jesus.

A tasting survey. Have a number of different fruit drinks and some drinking cups. Blindfold some volunteers and give them the different drinks to taste, asking them to name them. Record their opinions on a chart and then let them take off the blindfold and reveal the identity of the drinks.

Explain how we are going to hear about some people whose drink gave them a rather nice surprise. Have one of the servants telling the story. S/he can be holding a water jar and wearing appropriate clothing or headcovering to add to the effect. Whoever is telling the story needs to know the events well, and see it all from the servant's point of view. You can then slip in bits of hearsay about this man, Jesus, and comment on how you felt as he told you what to say and what it was that made you prepared to go along with what he told you to do. The aim is to help the children see what happened as if they were there as well.

Remind the children of the meaning of epiphany, and talk over with them what was being shown about God in this event. Read what John says at the end of his account. They had already decided to follow, and this sign backed up their decision.

Things to pray

Fill us up to the brim
with your Spirit, O Lord,

with hands horizontal like a water level, raise the level to the top of your head

and use our lives

open up hands and extend them in offering

for the good of the world.

trace large circle in the air with hands

Amen.

Jesus Calls Peter

Things to read

Acts 2:37-42
Luke 5:1-11

Things to do

Aim: To see the stages that Simon Peter went through when Jesus called him to be a disciple.

Pass it on. Sit in a circle and choose a leader. The leader does something (claps hands, crosses legs, winks, etc.) and this action is taken up by each person one by one, going clockwise round the circle. When it gets back to the leader, they start a new action for the next round. The point is that each person needs to be attentive to what the person sitting next to them is doing, and they then become the next in the chain of passing the message on.

Beforehand prepare a film clapperboard to snap shut as signs with the following headings are displayed. (The titles in brackets are written on the reverse.)

1. The night shift
2. Simon helps out *(welcome Jesus)*
3. Time to listen *(listen to him)*
4. The Maker's instructions *(see him in action)*
5. I'm not good enough! *(recognise who he is)*
6. Follow me *(follow him)*

Go through the story as if the film is being made, narrating it, with the leaders and children acting it out.

1. The children act the setting-out and pulling-in of empty nets through the night.
2. The crowd arrives, and Simon Peter offers Jesus his boat to sit in.
3. Simon Peter sits on the sand with the crowd, first busy with his nets and gradually listening more keenly. Give out an old net curtain for everyone to work on.
4. Jesus tells the fishermen to cast their nets again and they do so, with surprising and dramatic results.
5. Simon Peter reacts to the huge catch by realising Jesus' importance and his own lack of goodness.
6. Jesus shows Simon Peter that he knows what he is like and still wants him to work for the spreading of the kingdom of God. He calls him to follow and search for people instead of fish. Simon Peter follows him.

Display all the signs in order, then turn them over to show the titles in brackets. These lead on to the prayer time.

Things to pray

Give the children a set of five paper footprints, which they put down in a line in front of them. As you pray, move forward to each footprint in turn:

Like Simon Peter
I want to *welcome* you, Jesus,
listen to what you say,
see what you do,
get to *know* you better
and *follow* you all my life. Amen.

The Twelve Disciples

Things to read

Acts 13:1-3
Matthew 9:35-10:11

Things to do

Aim: To know the names of the disciples and why they were sent out at this stage.

Harvesters. Cut out lots of 'wheat', or scatter lots of long grass stalks all around the room. The idea is to see who can gather up most stalks between the starting and finishing whistle.

They have just been gathering in the harvest, and, as with the real harvest, they had to work hard to get all the harvest in. Where Jesus lived, in the area around Galilee, there were fields where the workers raced to get the harvest in each year. That's why Jesus used the harvest to explain the work his followers needed to be trained to do.

He could see that lots and lots of people were anxious and unhappy and discontented in their lives, and he wanted them all to know the happiness and hope of living at peace with God. They were a bit like all the wheat, ready and waiting to be gathered in to God's love. So Jesus said to his disciples, 'There are many people to harvest, but there are only a few workers to help harvest them. God owns the harvest. Pray to him that he will send more workers to help gather his harvest.'

At that time Jesus had his little band of disciples, who he was training up for the job. (Lay twelve cards with their names on face down on the floor. On this side only the initial letter is written.) See how many correct ones they can uncover. Put these in one line and turn over the others, one at a time, with everyone saying the name, before turning it over again. Now try to remember what this group of names was. Carry on until they have managed to name all the disciples, and all the names are face up. Then read through the whole list, in whatever order you point to them.

Jesus sent these disciples out to all the surrounding villages and towns to tell people that the kingdom of God was very near, and to heal any who were ill. This was good training for when Jesus had returned to heaven, and it also meant the disciples were working as a team with Jesus. They were sent out without lots of personal comforts, or extra clothes, or heavy luggage, and were told not to take any food or money with them, but accept the food and shelter they were given. That way the people would see that they were doing it just out of love.

And that's how we need to live, when we are working with Jesus in God's harvest.

Things to pray

Dear Jesus, here I am, signing on.
I'd like to be a worker in your harvest.
I understand that the only pay
is the joy of knowing
that we are doing your will.
Use me, Lord!

Saying Thank You

Things to read

2 Kings 5:1-19
Luke 17:11-19

Things to do

Aim: To look at the healing of the lepers and the significance of the one who said 'thank you'.

Musical chairs, or a similar game, where there is always an odd one out when the music stops. Today we are going to think about ten odd ones out, and one odd one out.

Two mothers, dressed up in head cloths, are in a village with their pots, collecting water from the village well. They pass the time of day, and then catch sight of the ten lepers in the distance, wondering who they are shouting to. One of the lepers, Jonas, is the son of one of the women and they talk about how sad they are that he can't live at home any more, and how badly he is missed, and how they have never stopped praying for him to be healed. They see that Jesus, the healer and teacher, is coming towards their village, and has stopped to listen to the lepers.

They wonder if Jesus could possibly be making the lepers better. They watch the lepers running away from Jesus and suddenly realise they are heading for the priest's house and are throwing off their bandages as they run. The women get very excited and soon they see some of the lepers running into their own houses in the village. They must be healed! The women start praising God, and are looking forward to Jonas coming back when they see him running all on his own back up the road to Jesus. What on earth is he doing? Then they see Jonas kneel down in front of Jesus. He is pouring out his thanks to Jesus, who is smiling and sharing Jonas's delight. The two women pick up their pots of water and go off to join them.

Things to pray

Put up all ten fingers and lower the fingers one by one as you say the first ten words. As you say 'Thank you!' you make a thumbs-up sign with one thumb, representing the thankful leper.

You always make us feel better.
Help us to say, 'Thank you!'

Jesus Stills the Storm

Things to read

Psalm 107:23-32
Luke 8:22-25

Please speak to me
when I am storming about
and calm me down as well. Amen.

Things to do

Aim: To get to know the story of Jesus calming the storm.

Simon says. This game picks up on the theme of authority – what Simon says goes!

Point out that in the starter activity you don't follow anyone's commands except Simon's because Simon is the one 'in charge'.

Now get everyone to sit so that they make the sides of a boat, apart from Jesus and his friends, who wait outside. The boat people can also help make the sounds of the lapping water and the storm. Tell the story as the children act it out, climbing into the boat, setting sail, baling out water and waking the sleeping Jesus. If the boat sides sway together as the storm increases you get a very realistic sense of being in a rocking boat.

Talk about how the disciples must have felt when they saw Jesus asleep, and when he calmed the storm. Point out that Jesus is often known as the Word of God. It was the voice or words of God which had brought the whole world into being at the very start of things.

Things to pray

Lord God,
when Jesus spoke to the storm
it calmed down.

Walking on Water

Things to read

Exodus 14:10-22
Matthew 14:22-33

Things to do

Aim: To know the story of Jesus on the water, and Peter walking to him.

If the weather is fine, have a paddling pool outside and some toy boats, or floating tubs to play with. Otherwise, have a number of washing-up bowls on plastic sheeting indoors.

One way of telling today's story is with a parachute. Everyone stands around the edge and the parachute becomes the sea, which can be made very still and calm, and various other stages of roughness to a roaring storm. Practise this with the children first, giving a clear signal for following the leader's instructions, so that they get good at all responding together. As you tell the story, use the parachute sea and its natural sound effects, with everyone shouting above the storm: 'Help! It's a ghost!'

Or you can get everyone making the sound effects of the storm and waves with percussion instruments, rubbing their palms together, tapping fingers on palms and using voices. For this have most people sitting in the form of a boat, and rocking in unison as the waves get worse, and a few, including Peter, inside the 'boat'. Then Peter can climb out of the boat towards Jesus.

Things to pray

Be with me, Lord Jesus,
through the storms in my life,
through the times
when I'm frightened or angry or sad.
Teach me to trust you with all of myself
through the good times and through the bad.

Who Is Jesus?

Things to read

Colossians 1:15-20
Matthew 16:13-20

Things to do

Aim: To know about Peter's confession of faith.

Who am I? Stick a picture of an animal or person on someone's back. This person turns round so the other children can see the picture. The volunteer asks questions to determine his/her identity, to which all the other children can only say 'yes' or 'no'.

Today we are going to hear about someone else. See if you can work out who it is.

Imagine you live in a village. Not far from your house is a sea, and your dad is a fisherman. Over the past year or so life has changed in your village because of a man who walks around the country with a group of friends. Everyone in your village knows about him. One person used to be so deaf she couldn't hear a thing, but she went to this man and now she can hear as well as you. Your next door neighbour couldn't walk very well, but he can now because this man made the leg better.

Every so often someone will come running into your village shouting that this man is talking by the lake, and suddenly everyone comes out of their houses, or stops what they're doing, and you all set off for the beach, just because this man is going to be there. And when you get there, you find crowds of other people from other villages have come as well, settling themselves down on the beach and the grass, looking towards a man who is sitting in one of the fishing boats. He doesn't look anything special. He's just wearing ordinary clothes, and he isn't shouting or waving his arms around or anything.

But everyone feels good when he's there. He has this strange way of making you feel important and special and yet able to be really yourself. People are kind to each other, making room for one another and helping the old ones sit down. This man seems to make you all want to behave well, just because he is so lovely himself. He tells stories, and gets you thinking about what life is really all about, and then he starts walking quietly around, praying with people, laying his hands on them and making them better, listening to them and comforting them. Some people have brought food, and often it all turns into a picnic, with the man enjoying the food he's been given, talking and smiling with you, interested in you.

And the day seems happier and brighter because the man has been to visit you. Who is this man – is it John the Baptist? Is it Elijah or one of the prophets? The man is . . . Jesus, the Christ, the Son of God.

Things to pray

Lord Jesus, I can see
that you must really be
the Son of God our Father,
because you speak God's word
and live God's love,
and there is no one else like you.

Jesus on the Mountain

Things to read

Exodus 34:29-35
Luke 9:28-36

Things to do

Aim: To get to know the events of the Transfiguration.

Pass the smile; pass the frown. Sit in a circle. Someone starts by smiling at their neighbour who then passes the smile on around the group. When it gets back where it started, try passing the frown around the circle. For a real challenge, start a smile going in one direction and a frown in the other.

Point out how the way we behave can get passed on to others. People who are happy often spread that around, and people who are gloomy and bad-tempered spread their gloom. The people who spent time with Jesus on earth were changed by being with him. Today we are going to hear two of those friends talking about a rather strange experience they had with Jesus, something they remembered for the rest of their lives.

Have two of the leaders (or two other volunteers imported for the occasion) being Peter and either James or John. You can have three people if resources run to this. They have just met up and are talking about what happened when they went up the mountain with Jesus and saw him shining as he prayed to his Father. Those who are chatting the story need to know the passage very well and talk it through together a couple of times beforehand. Think yourselves into character and talk about it as the real event it was, reminding one another of who you saw there, and what was said, thinking aloud your thoughts about what it meant, and why you were allowed to see it. The children will gain a great sense of immediacy if the conversation is informal but 'real'.

Have a mirror on the floor with several candles standing on it, and as the disciples get to the point when Jesus is deep in prayer have someone quietly lighting the candles. Nothing needs to be said about this, but the visual alongside the story will help touch their senses with understanding of the wonder of what was being seen.

Things to pray

Lord Jesus,
in your life we see the glory of God.
In our lives
we want to reflect God's glory
by the way we live.
May our lives
shine with love. Amen.

Jesus and Zacchaeus

Things to read

Psalm 32:1-7
Luke 19:1-10

Things to do

Aim: To learn about the fun of being forgiven and having a fresh start.

Bring a selection of chalkboards, chalk and dampened cloths, magic slates (which let you erase what you have written), white board, pens and cleaning cloth, and sand trays. Have a time of free play with these, so they can enjoy the satisfaction of drawing and erasing and starting again.

Talk about what they have been doing, and the fun of being able to start again whenever you make a mistake. Sometimes we make mistakes and do things that are wrong, and we wish they could be rubbed out as well as our drawings today.

Well, with Jesus, they can! Today we are going to hear about someone who met Jesus and was able to make a completely fresh start.

Tell the story of Zacchaeus using cut-out pictures on a background of carpet tiles or towels. The children can help place the houses and trees, and the crowd of people. As you tell the story, get the children to imagine what the other people were thinking when Jesus noticed the cheating tax collector, what Zacchaeus was thinking when he was noticed, and how he felt when he made a fresh start.

Things to pray

Lord my God,
you and I both know
the mistakes I make in life.
Please rub them out for me,
and forgive me all my sins
so that I can make a fresh start,
starting today.

Jesus Is Anointed

Things to read

2 Corinthians 2:14-17
John 12:1-8

Things to do

Aim: To become familiar with John's version of the story of Jesus' anointing.

Have a number of smells for the children to try and identify. Such things as an onion, grated chocolate, a cloth dipped in bleach, chopped grass, mustard, vinegar, and prawn cocktail flavoured crisps are placed in plastic boxes with foil on the top. Poke holes in the foil just before use.

Spread a cloth down in the centre of the group and lay it with bowls of raisins, grapes and crisps. Have two leaders telling the story between them, as if they are Mary and Martha or Lazarus talking over what happened at the meal. They hand round the food to people as they talk about laying on this celebration meal for Jesus and his friends. They remember how Jesus had brought their brother back to life, and how his friendship has made their lives so happy. Mary explains how Martha showed her love for their friend by serving a wonderful meal, something she's really good at, and Martha explains what Mary did while Mary acts it out. Discreetly spray some perfume into the air at this point so that the fragrance is all around. Mention Judas objecting to the waste of money, and have one of the sisters hinting at his real reason for objecting. Then the sisters recall what Jesus said – the way

he told them to leave Mary alone and stop nagging, because what she had done was very beautiful. She was preparing his body for burial. Mary and Martha can express their sadness as they remember all Jesus' suffering, but they end by reminding each other that even that terrible suffering was made beautiful by the love it showed us all.

Things to pray

No wonder people loved you, Jesus.
I'd love to have met you
and talked to you face to face,
and invited you to our house for tea.
I may not be able to see you now,
but I know you're just as much alive
as you were then.
Still loving us, still forgiving us,
still wanting us as your friends.
Thank you, Jesus,
for being the best friend ever! Amen.

Palm Sunday

Things to read

Psalm 118:1-2, 19-29
Matthew 21:1-11

Things to do

Aim: To look at why Jesus came riding into Jerusalem on a donkey.

If your church has a Palm Sunday procession the children will be joining in with this. Provide them with branches and flags to wave. Otherwise, have a procession with all the children and young people, making it lively and joyful with taped music, singing, dancing and percussion instruments.

With the children's help go over the events of Jesus' life from his birth in Bethlehem and childhood in Nazareth in a country which was ruled over by the Romans. Mention Jesus' Baptism and his time of testing out in the wild country on his own. Mention his job as a carpenter and his ministry, bringing out that he healed those who were ill, or unable to walk or hear or speak or see, as well as telling the people about the way God loved them. He talked about the king-dom of God, or the kingdom of heaven. This wasn't so much a place as a way of living – the loving way of living. As the events are mentioned, draw or write them along a time line.

The people wanted to make Jesus their king, but the kind of king they had in mind would lead them to fight the Romans and throw them out of their country. Was this the kind of king Jesus was?

Tell the story of the entry into Jerusalem, first practising these sound effects, which can be used during the story:

- Donkey – 'hee-haw!' and tongue clicking for a 'clip, clop' noise
- Jesus – 'Hosanna to the son of David!'
- Jerusalem – 'Holy city of peace' (whispered)
- Palms – rub palms of hands together to sound like the wind in the trees
- Crowd – 'Jesus! Jesus! Jesus!' in a chant

Things to pray

You laid aside your majesty,
gave up everything for me,
suffered at the hands of those you had created.
You took all my guilt and shame
when you died and rose again,
now today you reign
in heaven and earth exalted.

(From a song by Noel Richards
© Copyright 1985 Kingsway's Thankyou Music.)

Jesus Our King

Things to read

Philippians 2:5-11
Luke 23:33-43

Things to do

Aim: To explore the kind of King Jesus is.

What/who am I? Someone thinks of a person or thing, and the others ask questions to discover who or what it is. Only yes and no answers are allowed.

In that game we were finding out more and more about the person or object until we were sure we knew who or what it was. Write up the name 'Jesus' in large letters in the middle of a sheet of paper and write around it all the things we have discovered about Jesus in our lives so far. Already we know quite a bit about him, and we are getting to know him in person as well. Encourage them to keep on their praying every day, and see if any of them have still got a prayer habit. If we've got a bit slack, let's get that going again.

Today we are celebrating Jesus Christ as King. What kind of a King is Jesus?

On another sheet, with a crown with Jesus' name on it in the middle, collect their ideas about this, prompting them if necessary with suggestions of things Jesus isn't, like bossy, proud, or greedy. Then draw a cross going through the crown; the cross is a better sign for our King because all the things we've written are to do with love, which he showed by dying for us on the cross.

Read Luke 23:33-43 to remind our-selves of just how loving and forgiving our King is.

Things to pray

When I survey the wondrous cross
on which the Prince of Glory died,
my richest gain I count but loss,
and pour contempt on all my pride.

Were the whole realm of nature mine
that were an offering far too small;
love so amazing, so divine,
demands my soul, my life, my all.

Easter Day

Things to read
1 Peter 1:3-9
John 20:1-18

Things to do

Aim: To teach them about the first Easter.

Have an Easter egg hunt, preferably outside if this is safe and practical.

Invite a man to come along and be Peter, and interview him about who he is, and what had happened on Friday. Then ask him what happened on the next Sunday morning. Here are some questions to give you an idea:

- Good morning! What's your name?

- Now you're a friend of this Jesus, aren't you?

- I've heard that last Friday he was put to death by the Romans. Is that right?

- I expect you were there with him through it all, being such a good friend?

- Well, what happened on Sunday morning? We've heard a lot of confusing reports!

- Is it possible that someone could have stolen Jesus' body?

- Now hang on a minute. You're saying that Jesus is alive again for ever. That must mean that he'll still be just as alive in about two thousand years' time! Is that right?

- Well, thank you, Peter, for coming this morning to tell us this amazing news. We'll be looking out for Jesus. It's really good to know he's still alive!

Give the children a large letter (at least A4 size) to colour and decorate. These letters can be held up or fixed up on the wall or laid on the floor to make the message: JESUS IS ALIVE FOR EVER!

Things to pray

Christ has died. *(arms out)*
Christ has risen. *(arms up)*
Christ will come again! *(kneel on one knee, arms down, palms up)*

The Road to Emmaus

Things to read

Acts 2:14a, 29-32
Luke 24:13-35

Things to do

Aim: To know what happened on the road to Emmaus and the effect it had on the two disciples.

AA road map. Sit the children in a circle and label them (only verbally) in order, so that everyone is called one of three or four local roads. If you wish, you can include 'Emmaus Road'. When you call out a particular road name, those with that name have to change places. If you call 'AA road map!' everyone changes places.

Ideally you will be taking the children out on a short walk as part of today's teaching, provided this is safe and practical. Plan a route where you can move from Jerusalem to Emmaus and back; for instance, if Jerusalem is in the church hall, Emmaus might be the church porch, or the church garden. If an outside journey is not practical, then make your Jerusalem and Emmaus within the teaching area, but as far from each other as possible. Gather the children in Jerusalem.

Today's story takes place along a road – the road between Jerusalem and Emmaus. Luke was told this story by someone called Cleophas, who remembered all the details for ever afterwards, because he and his wife or friend – we don't know which – had never been so surprised as they were that day. We are going to walk where these two friends of Jesus walked, and find out what happened.

Explain that the two disciples were very sad that day because Jesus was dead and they missed him. They were also very confused and disappointed, because they had great hopes for Jesus being a national leader; they'd even thought he was the promised Messiah, but presumed they must have got it all wrong. They started off for home, which was seven miles from Jerusalem.

At this point gather everyone up and walk slowly along as you tell the next part of the story. Have one of the leaders who has been absent up till now join the group. This person takes up the story, from the point where Jesus joins them, and explains how the stranger helped the disciples to understand some of the prophecies from the scriptures which suggested that the Messiah would actually have to suffer and die in order to save his people, but that he would rise again.

By this time you will be approaching Emmaus. The first leader takes over the story, about the disciples inviting the stranger in, when he is making as if to go on, and the group goes into the Emmaus 'home'. The leaders produce some bread as they talk about the disciples having a meal together with the stranger. The second leader takes the bread and begins to break it while telling the children what the stranger did. The disciples suddenly realise who this stranger is – they recognise that he is Jesus, fully alive! During the excitement of this discovery, and the children guessing, the second leader discreetly leaves, and then the first leader tells how Jesus vanished once the disciples have realised who he is. They are really happy and decide to go straight back all the way to Jerusalem. (How far was it?) So everyone runs back to Jerusalem to tell the disciples there that they now know Jesus is alive – they've just met him!

Things to pray

The children can say this prayer as they walk along, perhaps with everyone walking round in a circle as at a skating rink. The leader can be one of the children.

Leader	Walk with me, Jesus.
All	Walk with me, Jesus.
Leader	Show me the way.
All	Show me the way.
Leader	Walk with me, Jesus.
All	Walk with me, Jesus.
Leader	Every day.
All	Every day.

Seeing and Believing

Things to read

1 John 1:1-4
John 20:19-31

Things to do

Aim: To know what it was that convinced Thomas and the others that Jesus was alive.

Place a few objects in a 'feelie bag'. Show the bag and point out that at the moment we can't tell what is in it. Now pass it around the circle. Each person has a feel and tries to identify the contents, but must not say anything. When everyone has had a go, each person in turn has a chance to name one thing they think is in the bag. Empty the contents so that everyone can see whether they were right.

Explain that in the last activity you could have told people what was in the bag, and they might have believed you and they might not. Would they have believed you if you had said there was a toothbrush in the bag? What about an elephant? Why are we more likely to believe some things than others? We use our common sense and our experience. If we have seen an elephant, we know that it wouldn't fit inside this bag, but a toothbrush would.

Today we are going to hear about someone who found it very hard to believe that Jesus really was alive. In fact he said this: 'Unless I see the nail marks in his hands and put my finger where the nails were, and put my hand into his side, I will not believe it.' (Have this written up in a large speech bubble, so that all the children who can read can join in with the words.) The person's name was Thomas, and he was one of Jesus' disciples and loyal friends.

Now ask them this question: 'How likely do you think Thomas thought it was for him to be able to see and touch Jesus' wounds?' (Have a temperature chart headed, 'Thomas thought it was . . .' with these markings on it: impossible, very unlikely indeed, most unlikely, unlikely, possible, likely, very likely, dead certain.

Different children can come and point to the level they think. (There isn't a right or wrong answer, but it gets them thinking!)

Next: 'Thomas wished it could be true, because he loved Jesus and missed him.' (Place this heading over the first with blutack.) Again, let various children come and point to the level they think.

Sometimes we believe things because we want them to be true. Who believes that (West Ham) will win their next game? Thomas didn't want to pretend to believe. He didn't want to kid himself. If it was really true that his friend Jesus was alive, then Thomas would believe it and be very happy. But if it wasn't, he'd rather face up to that.

A week later Thomas went with the other disciples to pray and eat together. Suddenly, there was Jesus standing with them, large as life and obviously completely alive! 'Hello!' he said. 'Peace be with you!' That's what people always said to each other when they met. (They can try greeting each other like this.)

Now for our next question: 'Jesus will ignore Thomas because Thomas hadn't believed that he was alive.' How likely is that? (Use the chart again.) Well, we are told that what happened was this. Jesus went straight across to Thomas, and said, 'Put your finger here. See my hands. Reach out your hand and put it into my side. Stop doubting and believe.' (Have this written large on another speech bubble.) So what will Thomas do now, do you think?

Last question: 'Thomas will only believe when he has touched Jesus' wounds to make certain it's true.' How likely is that? (Use the chart for their ideas.) Well, in fact Thomas found he didn't need to do all that. Just knowing Jesus was there was enough for him, and this time he said, 'My Lord and my God!' (Another speech bubble.) Jesus was very glad that Thomas now knew he was alive, and would be alive for ever. And he thought of all the people who would still believe even though they couldn't actually see him. Jesus was talking about you in that room nearly two thousand years ago. And this is what he said: 'Blessed are those who have not seen and yet have believed.' (Last speech bubble.) That's us!

Things to pray

With my eyes I may not be able to see you, Jesus, but I know you are real and I know you are here. With my hands I may not be able to touch you, Jesus, but my heart feels your love, your peace and your strength.

Peter Starts Again

Things to read

1 Peter 5:1-4
John 21:1-19

Things to do

Aim: For them to connect Peter's previous denial with today's commitment and commissioning.

Sit in a circle and go on a campfire-style 'lion hunt'. The journey to the cave – through short grass, long grass, sticky mud, water and so on – is repeated at speed in the other direction on the return journey. Today we're going to look at the way we sometimes have to go back the way we came to put things right in our lives.

Have a fishing net (such as a net curtain), some shiny paper fish, some driftwood and matches, and a mirror, explaining that all these come into today's story. Read the story from the *International Children's Version* or the *Good News Bible*, asking the children to listen out for when the objects are mentioned. This will help to focus their listening, and they will also notice that the matches are there as a sign of the driftwood being a fire, and there is no mention of a mirror. Explain that the mirror is, like the matches, a sign for something that is going on in the story.

Show people their faces in the mirror and point out that by doing this you are helping them to see for themselves what they look like. In our story Jesus is helping Peter to see what he is really like, and in our lives Jesus helps each of us to see what we are like as people.

Some things we know already. You probably know if you are a kind person, or if you worry a lot, or if you get easily upset, or if everything makes you laugh. You might already know whether you are good or bad at telling the truth, making up quickly after an argument, or cheering up your friends. That's good. Jesus wants us to get to know ourselves.

Sometimes people get frightened by what they find out about themselves. Perhaps they would like to think they were kind, but they find out that really they are quite unkind. Peter wanted to be the kind of person who would stick up for Jesus however dangerous it became, but he found out on Good Friday that he was actually a bit of a coward. Three times he had denied he even knew Jesus.

Jesus wanted to show him that he still loved him, and it was OK to be like he really was, so long as he didn't pretend he was different. That way Jesus could help him learn to be the brave person he wanted to be. Three times Jesus gave Peter the chance to say he loved him, so that the past was put right.

And Jesus says to us, 'It's OK to be the person you are. You don't need to pretend you're different. Together we can work on the things you find hard.'

Things to pray

Jesus, you're right.
There isn't any point in pretending
     with you,
because you know me as I really am.
I'm glad I'm me, if you're glad I'm me!
Let's work together
on those things I find hard. Amen.

Jesus Goes to Heaven

Things to read

Acts 1:6-14
Luke 24:44-53

Things to do

Aim: To see the Ascension in the context of the Resurrection and the coming of the Holy Spirit.

Cut several series of pictures from comic strips and fix them in groups on the walls, in random order. The children walk around the room on their own or with a friend or two, sorting the pictures into the right sequence. You can then take each group of pictures down in turn and put them in the correct order so everyone can check it against their own ideas.

Using one of the sets of pictures, get the children to explain why one picture couldn't possibly come before another. We have been picking up the clues based on what we know – a cat can't get wet before it has fallen into the water; a rocket cannot be in a thousand pieces before it has exploded. Today we are going to look at the order of events after Jesus' death, and see why they had to be in that order.

First there had to be the cross. (Place a cross on the floor at one end of the room.) It was through dying for us that Jesus set us free. This is how he saved the world with love. (Unwind a ball of string, starting at the cross, and taking it across the floor to a message which says, 'Jesus is alive!') Being the Lord of Life, death simply could not hold him prisoner for long, so the next thing for Jesus the Son of God had to be the Resurrection on Easter Day. (Unwind the string further, and place some broken bread on a plate on the floor.) Jesus needed his friends to know that he really was alive, so he appeared to them at different times, and often it was when he broke the bread that they recognised him. (Unwind the string a bit more, and place down a cut-out cloud.)

Once the disciples had begun to realise that Jesus could be with them without having to be seen all the time, they were ready for the next stage. Jesus had promised his disciples that he was on his way back to the Father, but that he wouldn't leave them on their own. Once he had returned to heaven they would be able to receive the power of the Holy Spirit. Jesus first had to go in glory back into heaven, so that (unwind more string to a picture of tongues of flames) the disciples could receive that power of the Holy Spirit.

Place a Bible, open at the Acts 1 reading, next to the cloud. Explain that this is how Luke tells us what happened on the day when Jesus was taken up into the glory of heaven. Read the account, using a version of the text accessible to children.

Things to pray

Jesus, you are our Lord and Saviour, reigning in the glory of heaven!
You were sent to love us to freedom and you did it!
Glory to you for ever.

Jesus the Word of God

Things to read

Genesis 1:1-3
John 1:1-3

Things to do

Aim: To know that Jesus is sometimes known as the Word of God.

Have a news session, with the children sitting in a circle and passing round a special stone (or Christmas decoration) so that the one holding it can speak while the others listen. This draws attention to the importance of listening to what is spoken, and helps to focus their attention.

Point out that we have all been speaking out, or expressing our thoughts. Then tell them you are going to read them something and you want them to listen out for someone speaking, and what the result was of the word they spoke. Read Genesis 1:1-3. See if they can work out that it was through the word God spoke into the darkness that light first appeared and creation could begin to unfold.

Now read them the first three verses from John. Can they spot the same idea? Show a picture from a Christmas card of the Nativity. And ask them a really difficult question to get their brains going: Which person in this picture spoke out, or expressed God's love for us all? The one who did this completely was the baby in the manger – Jesus! So in a way, as St John says, Jesus is the Word of God. He is God speaking out his love to us all.

Make them feel very impressed with themselves because today they have been doing a spot of something called Theology, and they've done it very well!

Things to pray

Word of the Father,
now in flesh appearing.
O come, let us adore him,
Christ the Lord. Amen.

PARABLES

Salt and Light

Things to read

Psalm 112:1-10
Matthew 5:13-20

Things to do

Aim: To look at how we can be salt and light in the world.

Together scatter tables and chairs around the room and then make the area as dark as possible. Everyone walks around, trying not to bump into any objects or people. Now switch on a light, or have a few torches available, so everyone can see where they are going.

Talk about how useful light is, as it helps us see so that we don't bump into things. It helps us to see where we are going. Now read them the section from Matthew's Gospel about light and salt, with parts of each displayed on sheets labelled 'Salt' and 'Light' as the words are read. Explain how light and salt are both things which allow good things to happen. Salt allows the full flavour of something to come out, and light allows people to see clearly so that they don't bump into things and hurt themselves.

So how can we be salt and light?

On the 'Salt' and 'Light' sheets, write down their suggestions. How can we behave so that people feel confident and happy in our company? How can we help to bring God's light into a frightening or wrong situation?

Things to pray

Help us, Lord,
to be salt in the world,
bringing out the best in people
by our love and respect for them.
And help us to be light in the world,
shining with your truth and goodness.
Amen.

The Seed of God's Word

Things to read

Psalm 65:9-13
Matthew 13:1-9, 18-23

Things to do

Aim: To know the parable of the sower and the seed, and its meaning.

Bring along a number of garden plants that have gone to seed, and harvest the seeds together in various labelled envelopes which can be taken home and planted.

Use some of the seed gathered in the starter activity, or seeds out of a packet, to show the children how you sow seeds in some earth. Then, as long as they have sunlight and water, they will grow. One of the stories Jesus told was about a farmer and what happened to the seed he sowed in his field. Explain how the fields were full of rocky places (put down some sheets of paper to represent these) and there were stony footpaths going across them (put down some footprints).

Show the children the way farmers sowed the seed at that time. They walked up and down the field, scattering the seed in handfuls to the left and the right. It didn't always land on the good, well-prepared soil, though.

In Jesus' story, some of the seed fell on the stony path, where the birds flew down and pecked it up. (They all fly across, cheeping, and pick up the seed on the stony path.)

Some seed fell on the rocky places, where it shot up very fast and then, because it didn't have deep roots, it shrivelled up in the midday sun. (They all crouch down and grow very tall until you show a big yellow sun, at which point they all shrivel up and fall down.)

Some seed fell among thorny weeds at the edges of the field. As it grew, the big tough weeds crowded round it so it never got going. (Name some children as wheat and some as thorny weeds. They all crouch down close together, and the weeds crowd the wheat so that it can't grow properly. No hurting allowed.)

Some seed fell into the good soil that the farmer had ploughed. And here the seed was able to grow up strong and tall, producing a fantastic harvest. (Everyone crouches down and grows up strong and tall, opening out their fingers to be the crop.)

And Jesus didn't tell the people what that story meant. He let them puzzle over it.

Put some quiet music on, and send the children to pick up all the seed that is on the floor, as they puzzle over what the story means.

Things to pray

Lord Jesus,
some of the things you say
are hard to understand.
But I do know one thing –
God loves us and looks after us
whether we understand or not.

The Costly Pearl

Things to read

Philippians 3:7-11
Matthew 13:45-46

Things to do

Aim: To know that the kingdom of heaven is like a pearl of great value.

Pearl divers. Scatter some shells or circles of white paper all over the floor. Starting from the edge of the rock (one side of the room), a few children at a time take a deep breath and 'swim' around collecting as many pearls as they can while their breath holds. They must return to the side of the room before taking a new breath.

Real pearl divers are often children, who have to swim deep down to collect the shells. There are only pearls in some of the shells, and usually they are quite small, but from time to time you can find a particularly large and beautiful pearl which is worth a great deal of money. They are sold by the pearl sellers to be made into necklaces and brooches. (If you happen to have a pearl necklace, bring it along to show the children.)

Jesus told a story about a pearl seller. In the market all the pearl sellers would have their trays of pearls on show, and everyone would go round looking at them, holding them up to the light, checking for faults, and haggling over the price. (Haggle over the price with either a child or another leader, until you come to an agreement.)

The merchant in Jesus' story was looking around the market for pearls to buy. (Have a child to be the merchant, and others to be selling their pearls. One is holding a velvet covered cushion and on it is a beautiful 'pearl' – a marble, perhaps.) The merchant went from one seller to another, testing the pearls in the light, and checking them carefully for faults. One of the sellers had a velvet cushion, and sitting all on its own in the middle of the cushion was the most magnificent pearl the merchant had ever seen. (Everyone draws in their breath in amazement at its beauty.)

This pearl had a glow of life about it, and it was large and perfect. The merchant knew that it was far, far more magnificent than anything else he owned, and he wanted to have this beautiful thing. But he didn't have the money to buy it. He thought of everything else he had; nothing seemed as precious to him as this perfect, glowing pearl. So he asked the pearl seller to keep the pearl by for him, and he went off and sold all his other possessions, just so that he had enough money for this one precious pearl. Then he came back with the money and bought it, and was completely happy with what he now had, because it was worth so much more to him than all the other things he had sold.

Things to pray

Knowing you, Jesus,
is the best thing in my life.
Nothing else is as important
as your love and faithfulness;
nothing else can give me lasting joy and peace.

The Wise and Foolish Bridesmaids

Things to read

1 Thessalonians 5:1-11
Matthew 25:1-13

Things to do

Aim: To know the parable of the brides-maids and its meaning.

As they come in, the children can make torches by fixing shiny red flames on to sticks with rubber bands or sticky tape.

Jesus was telling his friends about the future, and what would happen at the end of the world when he would come back in glory. He told this parable to help them understand. It's set at a wedding. If any of them have been bridesmaids or page-boys they will remember that there's a lot of waiting around to do at weddings, and the wedding in Jesus' story was just the same. Explain how in Jesus' time, the bride and groom would go to the bridegroom's house, and then come out in the evening for the party. All the bridesmaids would wait around near the bridegroom's house until they came out, so they could light the bride and groom's way to where the wedding feast was held.

The torches they carried were like ours – sticks with flames on the top. They soaked some material in oil and tied it on to a stick before lighting it, so they needed to have spare oil with them, ready for when the oil was used up.

In Jesus' story there were ten brides-maids waiting for the bridegroom. Five had plenty of oil for their lamps and five

hadn't been keeping themselves ready. When eventually the bridegroom was ready to go, the five unprepared bridesmaids panicked. 'Give us some of your oil!' they said. 'Ours is running out!' But the other five couldn't give their oil. If they had done that there wouldn't have been enough light from any of the lamps, so they sent the unprepared bridesmaids to buy some more oil.

By the time they got back, the bride and bridegroom had been led through the night by the lamps of the other five bridesmaids, and the whole wedding party had gone in to the feast. The five unprepared bridesmaids weren't recognised when they hammered on the door, so they missed out on the party, all because they hadn't kept their oil supplies at the ready.

Jesus said to his hearers, 'So you keep awake and keep prepared, because you don't know when the bridegroom will be returning, and if you aren't ready, you'll find yourselves shut out of the celebrations on the last day.'

He was talking about the time when he will return in all the glory of God at the end of time. And we all need to keep our lamps topped up with oil ready for that.

Things to pray

Give me oil in my lamp, keep me
    burning,
give me oil in my lamp, I pray,
give me oil in my lamp, keep me
    burning,
keep me burning to the break of day.

The Talents

Things to read
2 Thessalonians 3:6-15
Matthew 25:14-30

Things to do

Aim: To know the parable of the talents and its meaning.

I am the music man, I come from down your way. There are lots of instruments the music man can play, which are 'played' by everyone in this song.

Point out how talented the music man was in that song, able to play lots of different instruments. Today we are going to look at the gifts we have been given, and how God hopes we will enjoy them and make the most of them. Talk about the sort of gifts God gives us, such as being good at particular sports or skills, being thoughtful and kind, making people feel comfortable, helping them when they're ill, using money wisely, being able to work out answers to tricky problems, listening well, leading, or helping people make up after an argument. Some of us are given the happiness and security of a loving home, and others are given the gift of being cheerful even when life is difficult for us. All these things can be used to help the world.

Go round the group in circle time, with everyone saying, 'I'm glad God made me good at . . .'

Jesus told a parable about being responsible about our gifts, and using them, rather than hiding them away and ignoring them. As they will see, God expects us to make good use of whatever we are given.

Now read a children's version of Matthew 25:14-30.

Things to pray
Lord God,
thank you for giving us gifts and
    talents.
Help us to enjoy them and use them
    well
for the good of the world.

Real Wealth

Things to read

1 Timothy 6:1-10
Luke 12:13-21

Things to do

Aim: To look at real lasting wealth.

My aunt went to Paris. Sit in a circle. The first person says, 'My aunt went to Paris and she bought a . . .' They name something and mime it at the same time. The next person has to say this item followed by their own, and so on.

Lots of people put their trust in possessions, rather than in God. They forget that these can only last up to death, at the very most.

Tell the story of the rich fool, using the script below.

Narrator	There was once a rich man who had a very good harvest. *(Sound of running)*
Slave	Master! Master!
Rich man	*(Snoring; wakes up)* Oh! Yes – what is it, slave?
Slave	Master, we've filled all the barns with grain but there's still lots left.
Rich man	*(Laughs)* Well, well! So there's no room to store my crops, eh? Now what can I do about that.
Slave	Perhaps you could give some away?
Rich man	What! Good heavens, no! I know what I'll do. Slave – start building new barns – enough to hold all my grain.
Slave	Very well, Master; your wish is my command. *(Runs off. His voice is heard in the distance)* Come on, lads, get busy. We've got to build new barns.
Other slaves	*(Groaning)* Oh no! What on earth for, etc? *(Sounds of workers building.)*
Rich man	Ah, good, the new barns are splendid! Now I've got so much grain I can enjoy myself for years to come. I think I'll start with a feast. No more worries for me! *(Sounds of eating and drinking)* *(Cymbal, or saucepan lids)*
God	Fool! Fool! *(Cymbal)*
Rich man	*(Flustered)* Eh? Oh, my goodness, who said that? *(Cymbal)*
God	I, God, tell you that you are a fool! This very night you are going to die. What use will your hoard of grain be to you then? *(Cymbal)*
Narrator	So the man saw that getting rich did not make him safe and secure.

Things to pray

Thank you, Father,
for showing us a new way to live,
trusting in your love
and storing treasure in heaven.

Following Instructions

Things to read
James 1:22-27
Matthew 7:21-29

Things to do

Aim: To think about the need to change words into a way of life.

Divide the group into teams and have a set of instructions for each team. Each team is given their first instruction which they rush off and do, bringing back the answer before you give them the next instruction. The first team to complete all their instructions wins. Here are some suggestions for the instructions:

• Bring a list of signatures of everyone in the team.

• How far from the wall do you stretch if you all lie end to end?

• Stand in order of height/hair length.

• Bring the total number of fingers and toes in the team.

Draw attention to the way they needed to do two things in that game:

1. To listen carefully to what they were told.

2. To carry out the instructions.

That's very much what Jesus was teaching – how to listen carefully and then put what we hear into action!

Anyone who goes to dancing, or sports training, or is learning to play a musical instrument will know that the way to do it is to listen to what your teacher or trainer says, and then do your practice.

Jesus is our trainer and teacher, who tells us all about living.

Then Jesus told one of his stories to help us understand that the people who hear what he says and then act on it are like wise builders, who build their house on proper foundations of solid rock. (Build a brick house on a firm but well-protected surface as you speak.) Those who hear what Jesus tells them and yet do nothing about it are as foolish as builders who build their house on sand. (Build another house on a tray of dry sand.)

What is so wise about building on rock? When the storms of life pour down it will still stay standing. (Pour water over the house on rock.) When the storms of life pour down on a house built on sand, it's a different story completely. (Pour water over the sand so that the house built on it collapses.)

So the wise thing for us to do is to start putting Jesus' teaching into action so that our lives and behaviour are like strong houses built on strong foundations.

They can sing *The wise man built his house upon the rock* (CHB*) with actions of building (fist on fist), rain coming down (wiggling fingers moving down) and floods coming up (hands sweeping upwards).

Things to pray

Lord Jesus, I want to be a real follower
   of yours.
I don't just want to say it,
I want to do it as well.
Please help me to put what you tell me into practice this week. Amen.

*Children's Hymn Book, No. 200. Published by Kevin Mayhew.

Lost and Found

Things to read

Ezekiel 34:1-6, 11-16
Luke 15:1-10

Things to do

Aim: To explore the meaning of the lost sheep and the lost coin.

Hunt the coins. For larger groups, have several coins on the go at the same time.

Share your stories of losing something really important and then finding it again after searching everywhere for it. (Or you could pretend to have lost something and get everyone searching for it. When it is found you can draw attention to the relief and happiness.)

Jesus knew what this was like. Perhaps it was his mum or auntie who had once lost one of those coins from a marriage necklace, and he remembered the way they had all searched and celebrated.

Show the children a picture of such a necklace, or, if possible, a real example borrowed from your local Resource centre, and tell the story of the woman losing one of the coins. Use a real broom as you describe the sweeping of the whole house.

Explain that whenever one of us gets 'lost' – cut off from God – he too is really sad, and keeps searching and searching until he finds us again.

Things to pray

We pray for those
who have made wrong choices
and cut themselves off from God.

We pray for all those
who are living evil lives.
May all the lost be found again. Amen.

Forgiveness

Things to read

Psalm 103:8-13
Matthew 18:21-35

Things to do

Aim: To know the parable of the unforgiving servant and explore its meaning.

Help everyone to feel their heartbeat or pulse. Explain that we are going to do an experiment and find out what happens to our heartbeat when we do exercise. Then lead them in running on the spot, star jumps and frog hops for a while, or dance to some praise music. Now everyone feels their pulse again. Is it any different? What have we discovered? That when we move about fast, our heart beats faster.

The natural result of moving about is that our heart beats faster. What is the natural result of sitting in the sun? We get hot. What's the natural result of putting the plug in a washbasin and turning on the taps? We get a basin filled with water. What's the natural result of climbing into a swimming pool? We get wet. Lots of things happen naturally as a result of something else.

Wanting to forgive is the natural result of loving. It's what happens. God forgives us because he loves us so much. We're not always so keen to forgive when people have done things to upset us, and Jesus told one of his parables (his stories with secret meanings) about it to help us.

You will need three puppets, made from socks or paper bags as shown.

Give this script to three children to read, and sit them down behind a table placed on its side, so the puppets show over the top.

Narrator	In this story there is Mr Boss the master . . .
Mr Boss	Hello there!
Narrator	Servant Sam . . .
Servant Sam	Hi!
Narrator	. . . and Servant Ben.
Servant Ben	Good morning!
Narrator	Servant Sam had borrowed loads and loads of money from Mr Boss and one day Mr Boss called him in and demanded that the money should be paid.
Mr Boss	You owe me millions and I want my money back NOW! If you can't pay me, then you and your wife and children will have to be sold.
Servant Sam	Oh, Mr Boss! I haven't got the money to give you yet. Please, please, just give me time and I will pay it all.
Narrator	Mr Boss felt sorry for Servant Sam so he let him off.

Mr Boss	OK, Sam. I will let you off. It is a lot of money but you are free. You do not have to pay it.
Servant Sam	You mean I will never have to pay it?
Mr Boss	Never.
Servant Sam	Oh, thank you, thank you, Mr Boss! You are so kind. Yippee – I'm free!
Narrator	Servant Sam was very grateful and very happy. But later on he met Servant Ben who owed him a little money, and he got hold of Ben round the neck and shouted at him to give the money back.
Servant Sam	Come on, Ben, hand over my money. Hand it over NOW! I want it back!
Servant Ben	Oh, Sam, it's only a little bit of money, but I haven't got it to give you. Please give me time and I will pay it all.
Narrator	But Servant Sam wouldn't listen. He had Ben thrown into prison.
Servant Sam	Off to prison with you!
Narrator	When the other servants told Mr Boss about it, he was very upset and very angry, and he went to find Servant Sam.
Mr Boss	Sam, how dare you do that to Ben! You owed me loads of money and I felt sorry for you and let you off. But you did not let Ben off at all. So now
	I will throw you into prison!
Narrator	Servant Sam was kept in prison until he had paid every last penny.

Things to pray

Father, if you are so kind
and forgiving to us,
we need to be kind and forgiving
to one another.
Please help us.

The Rich Man and Lazarus

Things to read

Acts 3:1-10
Luke 16:19-31

We give you ourselves
for you to use
in helping them. Amen.

Things to do

Aim: To get to know the story of the rich man and Lazarus.

During a song, arrange for one of the leaders to come in wearing a hat and carrying a trowel, walk across the room and go out again. Don't draw attention to this; ignore it. After the song, ask the children if they noticed anyone coming in during the song, and what they looked like. The person comes in again, and explains that today we are going to hear about someone who didn't take any notice of the needs of someone he saw every day.

Use the children to be Lazarus and the rich man, the dogs, the angels and Abraham, as you narrate the story, either directly from the Bible (the New Century *International Children's Bible* is excellent) or in your own words. If you have a spare leader you can go for voice-overs as well.

After the story, talk about what the rich man had done wrong, and how his wealth had made him so comfortable that he didn't notice the needs of others staring him in the face. The children may have some ideas of how the rich man could have done it better.

Things to pray

Lord, we pray for the poor
and those who don't have enough to
  eat.

FOLLOWING JESUS

The Good Shepherd

Things to read

Psalm 23
John 10:1-10

Things to do

Aim: To look at what Jesus meant by saying he was the Good Shepherd, and the sheep door.

Give everyone a paper sheep to cut out and write their name on, and stick them all on a pre-painted hilly background with a shepherd standing in the middle.

Display the sheep picture and start writing the words to go underneath it, one by one: *The Lord is my shepherd*. As you write the first word the children repeat it, catching hold of the thumb of their left hand. With the second word they catch hold of their index finger and so on. Soon they will have learnt the whole sentence. Now point out that each of the sheep on the picture has a particular name. If we are all those sheep, who do they think the shepherd is? It's Jesus. Jesus called himself the Good Shepherd because he looks after his sheep (that's us). Go through the sentence again, hanging on to your ring fingers as you emphasise that the Lord is *my* shepherd – and that means John's, Abigail's, Thomas's and Ali's shepherd.

(Place a jagged sign called 'Sin' on the floor.) Jesus knows that bad and wrong ideas come to us sometimes in life, like attacking wolves, and he says he will fight off those evils to keep our bodies and spirits safe, if only we will let him. (Place a cross to 'cross out' the sin.)

(Place an open Bible and bread and wine on the floor.) Our spirits need feeding, like our bodies, and Jesus will feed us with God's words of love and wise help, often through our Bible reading, through the bread and wine at Communion, in the beauty of the world and through other people we meet.

(Place a compass on the floor.) Our spirits need guiding and teaching, and Jesus will whisper into our hearts the sense of what is right and wrong, so that we know, and can choose the best direction to go in.

(Place a phone on the floor.) Our spirits need friendship, and Jesus gives us that, too. We can talk with him about anything, anywhere, and be sure that he is interested, and has time to listen to us. And he gives us the company and friendship of other Christians to help us as well, which is very important.

Things to pray

The Lord is my shepherd;
I have everything I need.
He gives me rest in green pastures.
He leads me to calm water.
He gives me new strength.
For the good of his name,
he leads me on paths that are right.
Even if I walk through the dark valley
    of death,
I will not be afraid because you are with
    me.
Your rod and your staff comfort me.

(From Psalm 23)

Jesus the Way

Things to read

Isaiah 35
John 14:1-14

Things to do

Aim: To explore what it means to look at Jesus as the Way, the Truth and the Life.

Set up a narrow way to walk along. (It might be a thin strip of card, or two skipping ropes, laid on the floor.) Everyone can try walking along it without falling off and being caught by all the alligators (those who are not walking along the thin road!). If they are caught by an alligator (touching is quite enough) they are out. Alligators are not allowed to get them while they are on the road.

Bring along some newspaper pictures and headlines which tell of war and sad things, and introduce them, one by one, before dotting them around on the floor in the centre of the circle. Talk with them about there being so many sad and bad and dangerous things in this life, as well as all that is lovely and good. It is important for us on our Christian journey to know that this is true. There are lots of things to tempt us into doing wrong and unkind and selfish things. It is not easy to walk through life doing what is right.

Read together what Jesus says about all this: 'Don't let your hearts be troubled. Trust in God and trust in me . . . You know the way to the place where I am going.' Thomas said to Jesus, 'Lord, we don't know where you are going. So how can we know the way?'

Now take a length of string and wind it on a safe way between all the pictures and headlines, right across the circle, as someone reads the next sentence: 'Jesus answered, "I am the Way. And I am the Truth and the Life. The only way to the Father is through me."' Explain that Jesus was saying that he is like the safe path through a minefield; his close friendship with us all through our life is like a clear road for us to walk along to heaven. Give out separate words of 'I am the Way, the Truth and the Life' to different children and let them lay these words in order along the winding string 'road'. Then everyone can say them together.

Things to pray

Jesus, I know that you are the Way,
the Truth and the Life.
Let me walk safely each day
through all the troubles and
    temptations
by walking your Way
which leads me to heaven. Amen.

Counting the Cost

Things to read

Hebrews 12:1-3
Luke 14:25-33

Things to do

Aim: To be sure we know what it costs to follow Jesus.

Tower building. Collect lots of boxes and cartons, and sort them into sizes with price tags on them. Use Monopoly money and make the prices of the 'bricks' very high, so the children are dealing in hundreds of pounds. Issue each small group with a set amount of money and have a leader in charge of the brickyard. The members of the teams have to decide which bricks to buy with their money to stack up their tower. (No sticky tape allowed!)

Use two leaders or a leader and a child to act out the following dialogue:

Miriam is sweeping the floor when Alex comes bursting in.

Alex   Miriam! Miriam! Where are you? Oh, there you are! Listen, I've had a *really* good idea.

Miriam   Not another one! I was cleaning up after your last good idea for days.

Alex   Ah, the olive tree shaker, you mean. Well, I wasn't to know the olives and insects would all shake off into your bowl of flour, was I! Anyway, this idea is different, and it's *really good.*

Miriam   OK, dear, I'm listening. Tell me your idea.

Alex   A tower.

Miriam   A tower? What do you mean, a tower?

Alex   I'm going to build one! It'll be very high, so you'll be able to climb up the tower and check on all the sheep and lambs without having to go all the way to the fields! There, what do you think?

Miriam   Mmm, it sounds like a good time-saver, but there's one rather big problem.

Alex   Oh, really? What's that, Miriam?

Miriam   How are you going to pay for it?

Alex   Well, I've got enough bricks to build the first bit, Miriam.

Miriam   Oh, Alex, you'll look a prize idiot if you build the first bit and then can't finish it off!

Alex   Yes, I suppose you're right. Perhaps I'll go and sit under the olive tree and work out a few sums.

Then read Luke 14:28-30, 33. If we decide to join Cubs or Brownies, or start a new sport or learn to play the flute, we know we are committing ourselves to time and effort.

Following Jesus is a commitment, too. We have to be prepared to give it what it takes, whatever the cost.

Things to pray

Lord, prepare us to face all difficulties with courage and faith as we follow you.

Obeying Jesus

Things to read

2 Timothy 2:1-5
John 14:15-21

Things to do

Aim: To see obedience as a mark of love.

Square bashing. First teach the children how to stand to attention, to stand at ease, to about-turn right and left, and to march. Then line them up like an army and be a sergeant major, taking them through their paces.

Explain how, in the army (or navy or air force), everyone has to obey orders, and drill like that helps the soldiers get used to doing what they are told straight away. It just wouldn't work, where there are guns and explosives around, to have people who were not disciplined; obedience is a matter of life or death.

Most of us find it hard to be obedient – we would rather do what we want than what we are told! But Jesus can't use us as his soldiers in the battle against evil unless we are trained to obey him, like good soldiers obey their commanders. Jesus told his followers this: 'If you love me, you will do the things I command. The one who knows my commands and obeys them is the one who loves me.'

Jesus isn't getting hold of us in a half-Nelson and saying, 'Now listen you, obey me or else!' He would never, ever want to force us to do anything. He respects us too much for that. But he *is* saying, 'OK, you say that you love me and trust me as your Lord. If you really meant that, you would be doing what I told you, out of love and respect for me. If you just go on pleasing yourself, and doing what you want all the time, it shows that you don't really love me at all.'

He's right, and we can't get away from it. If we do mean it when we say we love and trust Jesus, then we'll have to get in training to be more obedient. At our Baptism this was said to us: 'Fight valiantly under the banner of Christ against sin, the world and the devil, and continue his faithful soldier and servant to the end of your life.'

There's a very helpful song for today called *To be with you* by Mike Burn which is recorded *(Kids' Praise, 96)*, so you could sing and dance along to it. Otherwise, finish with a couple of swiftly obeyed marching commands.

Things to pray

(To be said while marching on the spot.)

I love to be with you, Jesus,
so I'm going to do as you say,
I'll show that I love you and want to be like you
by doing your will TODAY.

(End by jumping to attention.)

The Proof of Obedience

Things to read

James 2:14-18

Matthew 21:28-31

Things to do

Aim: To know we have to choose whether to work with God or against him.

Beforehand prepare a number of pieces of drinking straw holding rolled-up numbers. Half these numbers (all of which are in the same colour straw) end with a 0. The children choose a straw and see if it has a 0 in the number. If it has they can have a sweet or a sticker. Draw their attention to the colour of the winning straws. Have enough winning ones for everyone to have one if they choose the right colour.

Talk about the choices we make all day long – what to have for breakfast, whether to brush our teeth or pretend we have already brushed them, whether to play football or chat with friends, whether to share our crisps or eat them all ourselves, whether to work hard or waste our time. Some of these choices don't matter much, but when they are choosing between good or bad, kind or unkind, then they matter very much.

One of the parables Jesus told was about two brothers. Their dad was yet another vineyard owner – there are a lot of vineyards in Israel (you could have a bottle of wine from that area to prove it) so that is why Jesus used them a lot in his stories. Today he would probably talk about owners of video shops or supermarkets. Anyway, the dad went to one of his sons and said, 'Off you go and work in the vineyard, son.' And his son turned round and said to his dad, 'No, I'm not going to.' But later on he changed his mind, and went.

Then the dad went to his other son, and said the same thing to him: 'Off you go and work in the vineyard, son.' This son jumped up and said to his dad (very politely), 'Yes, sir, I will!' But he didn't actually go.

Which of these two brothers did what his father wanted? When the children have told you, find the place in Matthew 21 and show them how they have just answered the question Jesus asked the people listening to his story. And it's the right answer. What is Jesus telling us all in this parable? Who is the father? It's God. Who are the brothers? All of us. When are we like the first brother? When are we like the second brother? What is most important to God – hearing us say we will follow him and do his work in our life, or watching us choosing to do something about it?

Things to pray

Lord, teach me to choose good, not bad,
to choose kindness, not cruelty,
to choose honesty, not lies,
to choose right, not wrong. Amen.

Carrying Our Cross

Things to read

1 Peter 4:12-16
Matthew 16:21-25

Things to do

Aim: To look at what it means to take up our cross and follow Jesus.

Follow my leader. The children can take it in turns to be leader, standing in front of everybody and doing various actions that are copied by the group.

Show a number of crosses – one that hangs up, one on a neck chain, and a standing one, for instance, and gather from the children the reasons we Christians have a cross in our church and often in our home, and round our necks as well. What happened on a cross that we want to remember? Why is that so important to us? Draw out the fact that Jesus on the cross shows us that he was willing to die out of love for us, so that we could be freed to live as God planned for us, in close friendship with him.

When Jesus was teaching his disciples, he wanted them to know that following him would not always be easy. When we follow someone, we do what they have done. Jesus was willing to give up his life out of love for us. So true followers of Jesus will be the same. They will be so full of love for other people that they will be willing to give up their own selfishness. And that is what the shape of a cross is: a capital I crossed out. (Draw this for them as you say it.) Followers of Jesus do not put themselves first all the time; they think of the needs of other people. They don't push other people around or want everything their own way. Instead, because they love God and other people, they are happier working together with one another.

Jesus does not try and pretend that this will be easy, because he knows we all want to have our own way all the time, and if we are in the middle of a programme we really like, we don't want to stop and help someone else, or change channels so someone else in the family can watch their favourite film. It takes a long time to learn to cross out our selfishness, but the more we do it, Jesus says, the happier people we will become, and it will make God very happy, too.

Things to pray

Jesus, I know I am sometimes selfish.
  (draw a capital 'I')
Please help me to follow you closely, crossing out the selfishness
  (cross through the 'I')
and living more lovingly.
  (look at the shape you have made)
Amen.

The Easy Yoke

Things to read

Psalm 145:8-14
Matthew 11:25-30

Things to do

Aim: To look at how being yoked to Jesus helps us.

Ask the children to get into pairs and fasten their ankles together with scarves. Everyone can try walking about three-legged, or you could stage a three-legged race.

Talk together about what it felt like to be joined up together like that. Draw out the point that it made us all learn to work together with one another very well, because when we worked together we got along really well, without falling down.

Now show the children some pictures from library books of oxen yoked together. Explain how farmers will train a young animal by yoking it up with a good, strong ox who knows what to do. That helps the young ox to learn. Also, the load is not so heavy if two or more animals are sharing it. (You could demonstrate this with two people carrying a handle each of a heavy bag.)

Get a broom handle and lay it along the shoulders of two children. They each hold it in place with both hands. Tell one child to be the leader, and see if they can lead the other child carefully around using the yoke to guide and support.

Now read to the children what Jesus said to all those who are feeling heavily loaded down in life, and they will be able to pick up on the way being yoked to Jesus helps us learn his ways and eases the loads of life.

What are the loads we carry in life? As you talk about some of these, you can pray for people carrying them in a time of intercession.

Things to pray

Jesus, in you I find rest and peace.
I can talk to you about anything –
my worries and my fears,
my happiness and sadness,
my anger and disappointment.
You always listen and you always understand.

Friends of Jesus

Things to read

Acts 11:1-18
John 15:10-17

Things to do

Aim: To explore the nature of friendship and what it means to be Jesus' friend.

Play some circle games, such as passing the smile or passing the hand squeeze, and place-changing. (In this everyone makes a drum roll with hands on thighs, and chants, 'Is it you, is it me, who will it be? Who will it be?' Then the leader calls out the category, such as those who ate Cocopops for breakfast, those who are wearing stripes, or those who have a sister, and these people get up and change places.)

Explain that Jesus told his disciples they were to love one another. The way other people will recognise that we are Jesus' friends is by the way we love one another. If we don't live like that, it really means we are not his friends. Who do you think can be one of Jesus' friends? Is it only those brought up to go to church? Or only the ones who don't have bad tempers? Or only the ones who can read the Bible? (They can think about this; we'll talk about it after the story.)

Tell this story from the Early Church of how Peter had to learn something about who can be a friend of Jesus. After Peter has introduced himself, and one of the leaders has welcomed him and asked him to tell the children what happened, the story can be read directly from Acts 11, starting at verse 5, providing Peter is really familiar with it and can read it with feeling. Otherwise, he can memorise the gist of it and 'chat' his story. It is so important that any reading of Scripture lives for the children.

After the story, go back to the question you left the children to think about, and in a circle, so that all have a chance to speak, share their ideas.

Things to pray

Jesus, you are my friend
as well as my Lord and Saviour.
Please teach me to be a good friend
to others
all my life. Amen.

Faithful Service

Things to read

1 Timothy 4:6-16
Luke 17:5-10

Things to do

Aim: To get to know the parable of the servant doing his duty.

Put on some music, and do a challenging fitness workout, including, perhaps, running on the spot, stepping, skipping, bunny jumps, stretching, and touching toes. Praise them for the way they kept going and kept trying, even when it was hard or tiring.

Like our fitness training session, life can sometimes be hard work – such as when we feel jealous of a brother or sister, or when we are finding it difficult to do the work at school, or when there are arguments and rows at home. Collect their ideas and experiences.

How does our God help us at these times, and what tips has Jesus got for coping?

Use simple puppets to act out the story that Jesus told about the servant, doing it the first time with the servant coming in and putting his feet up, and the master protesting that he can't behave like that because he's a servant, not the master. Then make a 'take two' sign and act the situation out with the servant being praised at the end for doing all the jobs. The servant can then protest that he was only doing his duty.

What does the story mean? Jesus says that we are not to expect life to be easy and perfect all the time because it isn't. We can expect there to be sad and difficult times as well as all the happy and easy times. And when they happen, we are to just carry on doing what we know is right, without grumbling too much. God will be there with us in all the difficult times, so we won't be left alone, and he will give us the strength we need to carry on.

Things to pray

Set out a train layout, with a tunnel (which can be a shoe box with holes at the ends), a gradient and some points. Start the train round the track as you pray:

When life seems an uphill struggle, Lord,

All: keep me on track with you, Jesus.

When we go through dark and lonely times,

All: keep me on track with you, Jesus.

When we have to make choices about how to behave,

All: keep me on track with you, Jesus. Amen.

THE GOOD LIFE

Choosing God's Way

Things to read

Deuteronomy 30:15-20
Matthew 5:17-20

Things to do

Aim: To see that the ten commandments (God's way) are choosing life rather than death.

Scissors, stone, paper. In pairs everyone counts, 'One, two, three, GO!' and then chooses to show paper, stone or scissors to their partner. Paper is an open hand, stone a clenched fist and scissors two fingers opening and closing.

• Paper wins over stone (because it wraps it up).
• Stone wins over scissors (because it can smash them).
• Scissors wins over paper (because it can cut it).

In that game we kept making choices, but we had no way of knowing whether they were going to be good choices or not. In the Old Testament God gave his people some rules to help them make good choices about the way to live.

Lay out ten objects to stand for the commandments, so they are easier to remember. Here are some suggestions, but choose whatever you think would work best for the children.

1. A figure 1, cut out of card. (Worship only the one true God and no other.)
2. An empty picture frame. (Don't make and worship pictures or models of God.)
3. A name tag. (Don't use God's name disrespectfully.)
4. A 'closed' shop sign. (Honour the Sabbath and keep it holy, resting from work on it.)
5. A photograph of a family. (Honour your father and your mother.)
6. A toy gun or sword. (Do not kill.)
7. A purse. (Do not steal.)
8. Wedding rings. (Don't steal other people's partners; be faithful in your relationships.)
9. Tape – video or sound. (Don't accuse people falsely or tell lies about them.)
10. Leaflets which advertise coveted items. (Don't keep wanting to have what other people have got.)

Go through the commandments in order, showing the objects and discussing the meaning as you go along. Then repeat them round the group, so everyone can use the visual clues to help them remember.

Things to pray

Whenever we turn away from you,
turn us back to face you,
so that we can live a lifetime
of love and truth. Amen.

As Loving as God

Things to read

Leviticus 19:1-2, 9-18
Matthew 5:38-48

Things to do

Aim: To know we are called to be loving and generous-hearted, like God.

Pass the ball. Stand in a circle with a ball – a large blow-up beach ball is good to use. If the children don't already know each other's names, go round saying these first. Then whoever has the ball says, 'Here you are, Laura', and throws the ball to her. Tell the children to make sure that everyone has the ball thrown specially to them, so that no one is left out.

Talk about the fun of giving presents to people, both the wrapped-up sort we enjoy giving at Christmas and birthdays, and the little everyday presents like smiles and hugs, a crisp from our packet, a sweet from our bag, or our help with a job. Whenever we give in this loving way, we are being like God because he does it all the time. He loves giving us good things to enjoy and use. Using the carpet tiles as a background, add some pictures of the presents God gives, like sun and rain, fruiting trees, animals, people.

Now show a chart with ten faces on it, arranged in two groups of five. Explain how instead of loving one another, we tend to love only those we feel are 'on our side' by being in our family, our gang, or our country. And this is what happens: an eye for an eye, a tooth for a tooth. (Keep blacking out eyes and teeth in a tit-for-tat way, till all the faces end up blind and toothless.) Now let's listen to the teaching Jesus gave. Read Matthew 5:43-45, and across the picture of the faces write: 'Love your enemies'.

Things to pray

Jesus, this loving you talk about
is HUGE!
I know I don't always want to do it
but I can see it's a good idea.
Please help me to be better at it. Amen.

Loving Our Enemies

Things to read

Romans 12:14-21
Luke 6:27-36

Things to do

Aim: To explore what it means to love enemies.

Play any quick softball or beanbag game in two teams, so they experience working against one another. In all these games each side is trying to make it hard for the other. Point out that in the game we are playing at being enemies.

Sit everyone in a circle and pass a card round with the word 'enemies' on it. As each person holds the card they say, 'An enemy is someone who . . .' If they don't wish to say anything they just pass the card on. The rule is that only the person holding the card can speak.

Draw all the ideas together, or record them on paper. Then place a card which says 'Love your' in front of the other card so they can see Jesus' teaching: Love your enemies. Surely that can't be right? We've just heard all these nasty things about enemies, and here is Jesus telling us to love them. How on earth can we do that? How can we love someone who's always out to get us, and hates us?

Check in the Bible and find that it isn't a mistake; it really says, 'love your enemies'. Read the passage from Luke together.

Ask the children to make their faces full of hate and bitterness. Get them to notice how hard the muscles have to work to do it. It's better and healthier for us not to make a habit of hating and sulking if we're upset, and God knows that. Perhaps they can remember seeing some older people's faces. If we are always thinking life isn't fair, and we hate and resent people, it will show in our faces as we get older. But if we get used to forgiving quickly, and putting the resentment down, that will show in our faces instead. It's right and it's sensible to take Jesus' teaching seriously, even though it is hard to do.

Have the three words of the teaching written on three balloons and learn the teaching off by heart by saying it several times, popping one balloon each time.

Things to pray

Forgive us our trespasses
as we forgive those
who trespass against us. Amen.

Putting Others First

Things to read

Philippians 2:3-7a
Luke 14:1, 7-14

Things to do

Aim: To look at the implications of Jesus' teaching about hospitality.

In pairs feed one another jelly or creamed rice pudding. Provide clothing protection!

Beforehand prepare two children to act out the guests at the party who are taking the top and bottom seats, and have to swap round when the host wants the lower one up at the top.

Talk about the way we usually feed ourselves when we're hungry, and give ourselves drinks when we're thirsty. When we were feeding one another we got an idea of what it's like to look after someone else, checking that they have caught the spoonful, and don't have drips down their chin.

Thinking of other people's needs is an important part of the Christian way of living. One day Jesus was invited out to lunch, and he noticed the pushy way some of the guests were making sure they had the best seats, nearest the food and drink and near the hosts, so sitting there would make them look important. Jesus didn't like what he saw. It made him sad that people were pushy like this, wanting to be more important than anyone else, and not thinking of other people's feelings. So he told them this story to help them understand a better way of living.

Now ask the children to perform the sketch they have prepared, with the rest of the children being the rest of the guests. Draw out the point Jesus was making about wrong values – being thought of as important shouldn't matter to us nearly as much as it often does. As Christians we are not to think, 'What's in this for me?' all the time.

Things to pray

Jesus, teach me to give
and not to count the cost,
to toil and not to seek for rest,
to work and not to ask for any reward
except the reward of knowing
I am doing your will. Amen.

Words and Deeds

Things to read

Amos 5:14-15, 21-24
Matthew 9:9-13

Things to do

Aim: To know about our calling to show mercy in our lives and be real in our worship.

Lying. Sit in a circle. The first person mimes an action (such as brushing their teeth) and everyone else joins in the mime. The person next to them says, 'What are you doing?' to which the first person lies, 'I'm blowing my nose' (or anything else that they aren't actually miming), and everyone says, 'I'm blowing my nose', while they continue to mime brushing their teeth. Then it's the next person's turn to start a mime.

In that game they were saying one thing and doing another. That's just fine in a game, but today we're looking at what can happen if people say one thing when they're talking to God, but do something quite different in their lives.

Tell the children to put both thumbs up each time they think something sounds good, and down if they think it sounds bad.

It all started with Jesus making some friends. (This is a thumbs up.) These friends led bad lives, cheating people of money, and working for the Romans. (Thumbs down.) One of these friends was called Matthew, and Jesus called Matthew to follow him and be one of his disciples. (Thumbs up.) Matthew was very pleased to be asked (thumbs up) and threw a party for all his friends to celebrate. (Thumbs up.) There was lots to eat and drink (thumbs up), and Jesus and his friends were really enjoying themselves. (Thumbs up.)

The Pharisees, who were the religious leaders, saw Jesus enjoying himself with these bad people and they were angry. (Thumbs down.) They went up to Jesus' followers to complain. (Thumbs down.) 'What does Jesus think he's doing, spending his time with these kinds of people?' they said. 'They are bad people, and it isn't right for a religious teacher to waste his time with bad people. He should have nothing to do with them!' (Thumbs down.)

Jesus heard what they were saying and came over to talk with them. (Thumbs up.) He wanted them to understand that God loves all people, whether they are bad or good. (Thumbs up.) He wanted them to see that he was giving these people the love and healing they needed. (Thumbs up.) So he said to them: 'Healthy people don't need a doctor. Only the sick need a doctor.'

But the Pharisees did not understand. (Thumbs down.)

Jesus told them to go and sort out what was really important to God – saying you love him but not showing love to other people (thumbs down) or saying you love him and loving those that he loves (thumbs up).

Things to pray

I want to worship the real, living God.
And I want my worship to be
not just an empty shell
but real.

Flourishing and Fruitful

Things to read
Psalm 1
Matthew 22:34-40

Things to do
Aim: To know the summary of the law.

Tape some lengths of wool to the floor, criss-crossing the circle where you are all sitting. Choose four or five people to cross the circle at the same time, walking along the lines. The rule to avoid collisions is that whenever you meet someone else, both of you get off the line, swap positions and carry on. Point out how useful the rule was; keeping it made life easier and better for everyone.

You will need a full sheet of blue sugar paper as the background, yellowy green hills, a blue river, a brown trunk and branches, green foliage and red and yellow fruit. As you talk, gradually the picture is built up, sticking one layer over another. The completed picture should look something like this:

In the countries where lots of rain falls all the year round, the trees have plenty to drink, so their leaves grow well and stay green in the summer. The tree grows lots of juicy fruit. In places where there isn't much rain at all, like this picture, the grass gets yellowy and dies in the heat of the sun. The trees can't survive either. *But,* suppose there is a river flowing through the dry grass (stick it on) and suppose a tree grows up right beside the river (put on the trunk and branches). The roots of this tree can drink up the water from the river, so this tree grows lovely green leaves (put on the foliage) and they stay green. The tree beside the water can grow so well that it starts to have fruit – lots of fruit (stick on the fruits). Even when there are times when it doesn't rain, this tree beside the water is going to be fine, and have lots of fruit for the people and animals and birds to eat.

In the Bible, we are told how to live in the very best way, like trees planted beside streams of water. The Bible tells us that the river we need to live by is this:

To love God, and to love one another. (Write this in on the river of the picture.)

Live by this, and we'll grow and live strong and tall, with lots of good fruit in our life. Read the summary of the law in Matthew, now that they know its outline.

Things to pray
Help us, Lord, to keep your law,
loving you with all we are,
loving other people too,
that's what we will try to do.

Slave or Free?

Things to read

Romans 6:12-23
John 8:31-36

Things to do

Aim: To learn about the difference between being slaves to sin and being free to do what is right out of thankful love.

Yes, your majesty! One of the leaders puts on a crown and robe, and holds a sceptre. (This can be a cracker hat, a curtain and a ruler.) She sits on her 'throne' and all the others are her slaves. She tells them what she wants done and everybody does it, first bowing down and saying, 'Yes, your majesty!' She might want to be fanned cool, given a can of drink, have it opened . . . and tested for poison, picked up, put down, or have a book brought and read and put away, or be scratched with a back-scratcher.

Collect together some pictures from library books which show slaves building the pyramids, or rowing galleys, making bricks or harvesting sugar cane. When you are a slave someone pays money for you and then owns you, as if you are a bicycle or a TV. As a slave you have to do what your owner tells you to do, and you don't belong to yourself any more. No one wants to be a slave, and even if you are lucky enough to have a kind owner, it's still hard to be owned like a thing, instead of being a free person, and slaves are often unhappy. It is not right for humans to be bought and owned like this.

Pin up a heading 'Slaves to sin'. When we are slaves to sin it is as if we are owned by sin, and spend our lives doing what our selfishness tells us to do. Give some examples of this, read by different children from speech bubbles of card:

- You want that big bit of cake, so take it quickly before anyone else can have it.
- Don't bother to clear up – you want to go on playing.
- Pretend you didn't break that door; then someone else can get the blame.

If we keep doing all these things, whenever we want to please ourselves, we are just like slaves to sin. But that way doesn't make us happy. We need some help to put things right, so we can be happy and free again.

Over the 'Slaves to sin' sign put up a long piece of paper with the word 'Jesus' written downwards on it, so that you have made a cross, with 'Jesus' crossing out the 'Slaves to sin'. When we decide to follow Jesus, and let his life fill ours, we don't have to live like slaves any more. We are free to see that being kind and thoughtful and honest *feels* good because it *is* good.

It's much better to follow Jesus and be free, instead of being a slave!

Things to pray

We pray for all people who are slaves to sin,
whether they are children or grown-ups.
We want them all to know you, Jesus,
and we want you to set them free,
so they can live good lives and be happy.

God's or Caesar's?

Things to read

Romans 13:1-8
Matthew 22:15-22

Things to do

Aim: To look at Jesus' teaching about giving to God what is God's and to Caesar what is Caesar's.

Price tags. Give out a selection of play money to each small group of children, and have some objects for them to 'buy'. Then call out a price tag: 'Here's a pair of scissors and it costs twenty pence.' The first group to come up with the exact money gets the pair of scissors. The group with most items bought is the winner.

If you have any old or foreign coins, bring them along and pass them around, and also show the children pictures of Roman coins from library books.

Remind the children of how the Pharisees were becoming more and more keen to get rid of Jesus, and how they tried to catch him out with a cunning plan. In order to understand the trap, they will need to know something about the Romans. Using the books, tell them how the Roman empire covered lots of countries. The Romans would fight their way into a country and take it over, ruling over the people there. They needed money to build the roads and market places, the aqueducts to carry water and the public baths. So all the people in the countries the Romans ruled over had to pay tax. Do you think they were happy to pay tax to the people who had taken over their country? No, they weren't. In fact they hated it!

Now that you know this, you will see what a clever trap the Pharisees set to catch Jesus out. They went up to Jesus with the crowds all around him and asked him a question (show this so they can all join in with asking it): 'Is it right to pay tax to Caesar or not?'

Now that was a tricky question. If Jesus said, 'Yes, it's right to pay tax to the Romans', what would the people who hated the Romans think? (They might think Jesus was not standing up for his own country.) And if Jesus said, 'No, it isn't right to pay tax to the Romans', what would the Romans do? (They would get him into big, big trouble.)

So what did Jesus do? He asked to borrow a coin (pick one up) and he showed it to the people. 'Whose picture is on this coin?' asked Jesus. 'Caesar's,' they answered. Then Jesus said this: 'Then give to Caesar what belongs to Caesar and give to God what belongs to God.' (Have these words written out and all join in saying them.)

Clever, wasn't it? The Pharisees had set out to teach Jesus a lesson and trick him, but Jesus ends up challenging *them* to give God the honour he deserves.

Things to pray

Great is the Lord who has made heaven
    and earth.
He is our God and we are his people.
Lord God of earth and heaven,
we worship and adore you.

Thirsting for God

Things to read

Isaiah 55:1-9
John 4:5-15

Things to do

Aim: To explore what we mean by 'thirsting for God'.

'What I really need is . . .' Split the children into groups and ask for things you really need which one person from each group brings to you. The first group to bring the correct object wins a point. Here are some ideas: a left shoe, a coat with blue in it, glasses on a nose, a clean tissue/hanky, a pierced ear, a surprise, a song, four legs.

Have a jug and pour out a glass of water. Talk about when we really want to drink a glass of water. The children will be describing (and therefore imagining) times they have been really thirsty. Show them some pictures of the land around Jerusalem so that they can imagine what it would be like living there. The people would know all about thirst and how it feels, and how our bodies long for water when thirst threatens our survival.

Listen to the prophet's words in Isaiah, inviting people to drink. What does this kind of thirst feel like?

When your body is thirsty, you need to drink water. When your spirit is thirsty for goodness, right and truth in life, you need to drink in God's Spirit.

How do you know when you're thirsty for God?

Draw on a large glass: 'I need you in my life, Lord God'. When we come to God and say, 'I need you in my life, Lord God', we are telling God we are thirsty for him. Whenever we notice something that isn't right and fair, and want to put it right, we are thirsty for God.

Whenever we see news on television that makes us sad, and we start wishing that people were not so cruel and greedy, and that people didn't have to die from dirty water or starvation, we are thirsty for God.

Whenever we want to be more loving, more honest, more trustworthy, or braver at standing up for what's right, then we're thirsty for God.

So . . . how do we drink?

Draw a well.

You pray. Get in touch with the 'water' supply which in this case is God. Tell him about your thirst; cry to him for the people you feel sorry for. And remember that the God you are talking to is real, alive, and able to quench your thirst.

Things to pray

Waiting for your Spirit.
   kneel with hands palms up, heads bowed; raise head and look up
Thirsty for your Spirit.
   cup hands and bring to mouth to 'drink'
Touching us, Lord, as we pray;
   touch fingertips together
filling our lives with you again,
   stretch out arms with palms up
fall on us, Lord, as we call on you.
   slowly raise arms upwards

This can be said slowly to a quiet music background.

Moving On

Things to read

Genesis 12:1-4a
Hebrews 11:8-10

Things to do

Aim: To know that when Abram was called, he trusted God and went.

Follow my leader. Put on a children's praise tape and have different children leading the line with everyone following the leader in both method and direction.

Talk about moving house and have everyone miming the furniture removal, packing and unpacking. Share in the group anyone's memories about how they felt when they moved and saw their home being emptied, and the new one filling up. Help them to sense that moving is quite an upheaval, often with some sadness at what we are leaving behind, but excitement at what we are moving on to. Pick up on the fear and adventure of going forward into the unknown.

Now drape a large cloth over some upturned basins to make a hilly land-scape, and tell them about Abram, whose name God later changed to Abraham (marked on the landscape with a cardboard question mark), living happily settled when God called him to uproot and move on into the unknown. Describe the gathering, packing and moving, with the children making the noises of all the sheep, goats, cows, children (la, la, la) and grown-ups (natter, natter, natter) as the cross is moved over the landscape – rather like the wartime charts of progress. All the time Abram kept listening to God and checking where they should all be going. He trusted God completely. When we live closely in touch with God, and go along with his ideas, even if they take us into the unknown, we are living by faith – faith in a loving God who can be trusted.

Things to pray

Lord God, here is my life!
Lead me your way
and I will follow you
wherever and however you want.
Amen.

Imagining Heaven

Things to read

1 Corinthians 15:35-44, 49
Luke 20:27-38

Things to do

Aim: To stretch our minds to imagine things beyond our physical sight.

Put on some praise music on tape, and do lots of strenuous stretching exercises to the music, till their bodies are well and truly stretched.

Explain that we have been stretching our bodies and now we are going to stretch our minds as well. (Don't rush this journey – shut your own eyes and actually imagine it as you direct them and that will get the timing right.) Get them to shut their eyes and imagine their town all around them . . . and beyond that all the countryside stretching out to the sea all around them . . . imagine the round world curving away from where they are sitting so they are riding on the ball-shaped planet earth through space, going slowly round the brilliant sun. Take them on a speeded up reverse journey to end up back in (St Andrew's) hall, where they can open their eyes.

Even though we don't usually think about it or imagine it, we are actually doing that journey all the time! We really are perched on the outside of a planet, riding through space around the sun.

Jesus liked to get people to stretch their minds. There is so much that we can't see because it's too huge, or too minute, or simply invisible. We can't see heaven but Jesus told his friends that there definitely is life after death,

and when we die we will know exactly what it is like.

For the moment, though, while we live bound by things like time and space, we can only imagine how wonderful and brilliant heaven will be.

Some people, both now and then, didn't believe in life after death. They came to Jesus and asked him a tricky question. (You can either use children or lego-type people for this)

There was this woman (choose a girl to stand up) and she got married (choose a boy to stand). Then the husband died (boy falls down) so she married someone else (another boy stands up) . . . Carry on for seven husbands. Now at the resurrection (all the dead husbands stand up again), who is the woman going to be married to? (The girl pretends to look very puzzled.)

Let everyone sit down again. The people asking the question thought Jesus would have to agree that life after death was a silly idea. But he didn't. Jesus told them that they were expecting life in heaven to carry on in just the same way as life on earth, but it's not like that. In heaven there won't be things like who's married to whom, because we will be like angels, just happy to be God's children.

Things to pray

And our eyes at last shall see him
through his own redeeming love.
For that child, so dear and gentle,
is our Lord in heaven above.
And he leads his children on
to the place where he is gone.

PROPHETS

Elijah and the Prophets of Baal

Things to read

1 Kings 18:20-39
James 5:13-20

Things to do

Aim: To learn about the prophets' competition and the value of example in spreading the faith.

Have a beat-the-clock activity, where each person tries the same challenge and the one with the quickest time is the winner. Activities might be dressing up in thick gloves and eating a mini chocolate bar with a knife and fork, or transferring dried peas from one container to another using a straw.

Tell the children that today we are going to hear about another competition – rather an unusual one. One of the children can be Elijah, who can be dressed in a tunic and rope belt. Others are the prophets of Baal. The rest of the children are the crowd who came out to watch. As you tell the story, the children act it out. Give someone a tin sheet to rattle when the lightning falls, and have someone primed to take a flash photo at the same time, so the sudden bright light surprises the actors as well as the people in Elijah's time. Everyone can shout the words 'The Lord is God! The Lord is God!' at the end.

Things to pray

Dear Jesus,
we pray for those
who have not heard of you
and do not know you.
Give us the opportunity
to share the good news
with someone today. Amen.

Elijah and Naboth's Vineyard

Things to read
1 Kings 21:1-21a
Psalm 5:1-8

Things to do
Aim: To get to know the story of Naboth's vineyard and its implications for them.

Sit in a circle. Each person in turn says three things about someone in the circle (only positives allowed), and everyone guesses who it is. Each person can only be described once, which means that everyone gets a turn to be described. Or play 'Stuck in the mud', which is a kind of 'tag'. When caught, you stand with arms and legs apart, stuck in the mud, unless someone crawls between your legs to set you free again.

Tell the story with different children acting it out as it is narrated. Jezebel's letter can be written out (simplifying it for your group) and Jezebel can read it out. Balls of white paper can be thrown as stones, and simple costumes worn (such as crowns and cloaks for the King and Queen, tea-towel headdresses for Naboth and his accusers, and a piece of rough cloth for Elijah.

Things to pray
Talk about our need to recognise and admit to God the times when we let him down by our unloving, selfish behaviour, knowing that he is able to forgive us.

Lord God,
thank you for helping me do good
    today,
when I . . .
I am sorry that I let you down
and hurt others
when I . . .
Please forgive me
and help me put it right.
Thank you, Lord God,
for forgiving me!

Isaiah and Jesus

Things to read

Isaiah 9:1-7
Matthew 4:12-17, 23-25

Things to do

Aim: To see that Isaiah's prophecy is fulfilled in Jesus.

Use this puzzle which contains two solutions at once:

CLUES
1. The capital city of Judea.
2. We listen with these.
3. A prophet from Jerusalem.
4. It will come, but hasn't yet.
5. What God can do for all captives.
6. Who fulfilled Isaiah's words? (The answer is already there, but we might not have understood it before.)

SOLUTION
```
          6.
1.    J E R U S A L E M
2.    E A R S
3.  I S A I A H
4. F U T U R E
5.    S E T   F R E E
```

Use a length of string as a time line to help the children understand the time scale. Have today's date hung at one end, Abraham at the other, Jesus in the middle. Then hang Isaiah's name about two-thirds of the way along from Abraham to Jesus.

Explain that a prophet is someone who speaks out God's Word. Sometimes, but not always, this will mean telling people about things which are going to happen. Isaiah was a prophet who spoke out God's Word in Jerusalem about 740 years before Jesus was born. He told the people of Israel about the fair and good way of living that God expected from his people, and looked forward to a time when God's light would shine out all over our world which is so often darkened with evil and unfairness. (Collect suggestions about some of the evil and unjust things that happen.)

Read the section of Isaiah's prophecy which is today's reading, and then find on a map the places mentioned. Now for a question: Who do they know about who did walk about Galilee bringing light into people's lives? Jesus did! Read the passage from Matthew and see if they can spot the bit from Isaiah.

Things to pray

Thank you, Lord, for using Isaiah
to help us recognise Jesus
as your Son.
Thank you for making it possible
for us all to be free. Amen.

Amos and the Plumb Line

Things to read

Amos 7:7-9

James 2:1-13

Things to do

Aim: To think about measuring our lives against God's plumb line.

Have some tape measures and get the children measuring each other and recording the results on a length of string to see how far our group would stretch if we put them end to end.

It's amazing what you discover when you start measuring! Explain that today we're going to look at another kind of measure. We now know how we measure up in metres and centimetres, but what about God's measuring stick of love? Introduce the children to Amos, who has come to tell us about something God showed him. What was it, Amos?

Amos greets the children and tells them he comes from the southern part of Israel. He could see that the people in the northern part were treating their poor people really unfairly, and not caring about anyone who wasn't able to earn lots of money. And they were not bothering to worship the true God either; they were playing around with other things they called gods. He shows the children a plumb line and asks them if they know what it is. He tells them how God showed him a crooked wall, and he was able to measure the wall against the straight vertical of the plumb line and check whether it was straight or not. And he had found that the people of Israel were like a crooked wall against God's plumb line of fair treatment, loving care and respect for everyone, however poor.

Amos was the one God asked to go and tell the people that their lives and their country needed straightening out, and fast! But they didn't listen to him. They just got angry with him.

Thank Amos for coming, and ask him to remind them of what God's plumb line is, so we can measure ourselves against it and check whether we're straight and level enough. Amos tells them: 'Love the Lord your God with all your heart and with all your mind and with all your strength. And love your neighbour as yourself.'

You can all sing this with actions to remind you, to the tune of *London's burning*:

You shall love the Lord your God with
all your heart and all your mind and
all your strength! All your strength!
And love your neighbour,
and love your neighbour.

Things to pray

Lord God,
help me to notice
when other people need my help,
and remind me to do
what I can to help them. Amen.

John the Baptist

Things to read

Malachi 3:1-4
Luke 3:1-6

Things to do

Aim: To understand that John was the prophesied forerunner to prepare the people for the Messiah.

Advance notice. Have a selection of posters and flyers for local events (the local press usually drops several on your floor as you open the paper each week). Have some with pictures to help non-readers. Have the posters at different places on the walls and give the children a minute to walk round and look at them. Then have everyone in the centre. Call out: 'Did you know there was going to be a circus next Saturday?' The children run to the appropriate poster.

Beforehand prepare a poster that says: 'Good news – don't miss it! The Messiah is coming!' and a sign with a string attached saying 'John the Baptist'.

Explain that the people of Israel were waiting for the day when the Messiah would appear on earth. (Display the poster.) Everyone can shout the message together. The name 'Messiah' means 'the chosen one' or 'the Christ'. But God didn't rely on posters: he went for a better idea. He went for a personal messenger.

At this point one of the leaders interrupts to say that she wants to give advance notice of a children's Christmas party/carol singing (or whatever exciting event you have planned for the near future). The excitement generated by this will enable you to show how effective it is to have a personal messenger. Explain that the name of the personal messenger God chose was John, known as John the Baptist. (Hang the notice round the messenger's neck.)

What was John's message?

God told John to tell the people that to get ready for the coming Messiah, they needed to put their crooked lives straight. That meant sorting out all lying and cheating, all cruel and unkind behaviour, all mean and selfish living. This turning away from sin is called 'repentance'. As a sign that their sins had been forgiven, John baptised the people in the water of the River Jordan. The people felt happy and free.

Things to pray

Have everyone standing in a space facing the same direction. Whenever the leader says *Turn us round* the children turn around and continue with the prayer.

Father, whenever we are wanting our own way,
Turn us round to think of other people.
Whenever we know we are not being honest,
Turn us round to speak the truth.
Whenever we find ourselves being greedy,
Turn us round to share with others.
Thanks for helping, Lord.
Amen.

PRAYER

Stop and Listen

Things to read

Psalm 131
Luke 10:38-42

Things to do

Aim: To look at the importance of listening to God.

Sit in a circle, with one blindfolded person in the centre. Another person creeps round the outside of the circle with a jangly set of keys. The blindfolded person points to where the person has got to. If they are right they take the keys and a new person is blindfolded.

Begin with a sketch to express the busy nature of our lives. It will need to be prepared beforehand using one or two of the children. An alarm clock rings and the children dash in with dressing-gowns and teddies. They pretend to eat their breakfast really quickly, and grab books and pencil-case for school. They dash back in for lunch-boxes, and out, back for football kit or equivalent, and out, back for swimming gear, and out, back for violin or equivalent, and out, back to sit and watch television and eat something, and out, in wearing dressing-gowns and teddies again, and out.

Talk about what the children do on each day of the week and how nice it is to be able to do all these things, but how important it is to stop and spend quiet times every day with God. Have the children acting out the Martha and Mary story, bringing out the need to get the listening times right so that all the practical doing falls properly into place.

Things to pray

Here I am, Lord.
I have come to spend some time with you,
to sit at your feet and be quiet with you.

Persistent Prayer

Things to read

Genesis 32:22-31
Luke 18:1-8

Things to do

Aim: To learn about perseverance in prayer.

The separate letters for 'Regular' and 'Prayer' (different colours for each) are hidden around the room, and the children sent to hunt them out. They persevere until they have all the letters and can sort them out into the words.

Use the sketch below to introduce the parable of the woman pestering the judge for her rights.

Woman Knock, knock.
Judge Who's there?
Woman Winnie.
Judge Winnie who?
Woman Winnie you going to do something about that money I was cheated of?
Judge Oh don't worry, that case will be coming up very soon. Now if you don't mind, it's my day off and I'm going to play golf.
(Sign held up saying 'Next day')
Woman Knock, knock.
Judge Who's there?
Woman Winnie.
Judge Winnie who?
Woman Winnie you going to do something about . . .
Judge OK, you don't have to say all that again. I remember. I'll deal with it, madam. Leave it to me. *(Aside)* But not yet because I'd rather watch telly and have a snooze.
Woman Knock, knock.
Judge *(Sounding sleepy)* Who's there?
Woman Winnie.
Judge Winnie who? *(Aside)* Oh, hang on, I won't ask! I don't know, there's no rest for the wicked. Wretched woman, I'd better do what she asks or I'll never get any peace! *(Shouts)* All right, Winnie, you win. I'll come with you and sort it out *now*!

Point out that Jesus was saying, 'If even a lazy old judge like that eventually listened to the woman, we can be certain that our loving God will listen to us straight away every time, and answer our prayer.' Sometimes his answer might be that we have to wait, or that what we are asking for wouldn't help us as much as we think it would.

Have an alarm clock, a knife and fork and spoon, and a toothbrush and toothpaste.

Set them down and talk about these as being the times to remember to pray.

Things to pray

Use the symbols from the teaching.

Lord God, I want to keep in touch with
   you all through the day.
Help me to remember that in the
   morning *ring the alarm*
before I eat *clash the knife and fork*
and before I go to sleep *brush teeth*
I can talk to you and know you are
   listening.

Acceptable Prayer

Things to read
Psalm 65
Luke 18:9-14

Things to do

Aim: To get to know the parable from Luke 18:9-14 and learn about being right with God.

A 'getting it right' game, such as sticking the tail on the donkey, blindfold, or using some conkers to roll on to a board with numbered squares on it. Where your conker lands is your score.

Explain that Jesus found some people he was with were always looking down on others, and making out they were much better than everyone else. They seemed to have forgotten that they owed their whole life to God. Jesus didn't like to see that, and it made him sad. So he told them this story to show them how they were behaving, hoping it would make them realise what they were doing and try to change.

Use simple puppets, made out of wooden spoons or spatulas, to tell the story. The pictures below will help you with the expressions. Then talk about which one of the two went home right with God, and why. Reinforce that we all depend on God for our life, and everything comes from him. Read Psalm 65:9-13 and enjoy celebrating our love for our wonderful God.

Things to pray
You know us, Lord,
so we can't pretend with you.
You shower us with blessings
like a shower of rain;
you give us your power
to make us grow more loving
all through our lives.

The Lord's Prayer

Things to read
Acts 4:23-31
Matthew 6:5-15

Things to do
Aim: To look at the meaning of the Lord's prayer.

Play a game of hide and seek, or sardines, or look for a hidden object, with clues of 'hotter' or 'colder' only being given if they are asked for.

Jesus often used to go off on his own to talk things over with his Father in heaven and listen to his Father's advice. Sometimes they would just be quiet in one another's company. These times helped Jesus have the wisdom and energy he needed to do his work, as we mentioned last week.

His followers could see how useful those times were to Jesus, and they wanted to do it themselves but they didn't know how to. So they asked Jesus to teach them all how to pray. And this is what Jesus suggested they did.

1. Remember that God is your Father in heaven, and that he is holy.

2. Ask for the kingdom of God to come, and God's will to be done.

3. Ask for enough to eat and for your needs for the day.

4. Ask God to forgive your sins, just as you have forgiven people who have upset you.

5. Ask God to lead you safely through temptation and out of evil.

Have them written up on separate cards, and answer any questions about each one as you go along. Jumble them up and invite a couple of children to put them in the right order again. Then have someone reading each one out, and a pause for everyone to do what the card says. Introducing them to the meaning like this, before the traditional words, will prevent understanding being blocked by familiar but un-digested words.

Now see if any of them know the traditional form of this teaching, known as the Lord's Prayer. Teach them these actions to do as they say it, to make sure they are praying, and not just reciting some instructions.

Our Father
in heaven,
hallowed be your name.
Your kingdom come,
your will be done on earth (Look down)
as it is in heaven. (look up)
Give us today our daily bread (cup hands)
and forgive us our sins
as we forgive those
who sin against us.
Lead us not into temptation
but deliver us from evil.
For the kingdom, the power
and the glory are yours,
now and for ever. Amen. (Move arms slowly upwards and raise heads at the same time)

Things to pray
Use the Lord's Prayer with actions.

Wants and Needs

Things to read

Isaiah 55:1-3a
John 6:2-14, 25-35

Things to do

Aim: To know that Jesus knows our needs and provides for us.

What do I need? One of the children is given an identity or work label, such as postman or ice-cream seller. The others have to work out the identity by asking them what they would need to do this job of work.

Have a number of cards with these words on, illustrated simply, to help with reading: food, air, rest, sleep, hobbies, friendship, water, shelter, fashionable clothes, love, air, TV, chocolate, exercise, God. Have two heading cards: 'Wants' and 'Needs'.

Working together, decide which of these are wants and which are needs. This will mean looking at the things we actually need to survive and the things we think we need but which are only really extras, however nice they are. Sometimes people don't realise what they really need.

Really they need sleep but because they don't want to waste their time sleeping, they have a strong cup of coffee to keep them awake. That's OK sometimes, but if we start to live like it all the time it's bad for us. Really they need to feel loved, but instead of going to God and getting the love they need, they eat loads of sweets to comfort themselves, or drink loads of beer. And if they do this all the time it's bad for them.

(Place a piggy bank on the floor.) Sometimes we get let down or cheated by things we bought because we thought we wanted them and then found they didn't make us as happy as we hoped they would. Sometimes people think that being rich will make them happy, but real, lasting happiness doesn't come from being rich or having lots of things. Real happiness comes from God's love, which you don't even have to save up for, because he gives it to us free. However rich you are and however poor you are, God's love is free and will give you what you really need as a human being. It doesn't cheat you or let you down; it feeds you, just as a good meal feeds your body.

Things to pray

The Lord is my shepherd,
there is nothing else I need.
He leads me and he feeds me
all the days of my life.
O Lord, my shepherd,
you are all I need.

THE CHURCH AND ITS MISSION

Pentecost

Things to read

Acts 2:1-21
John 20:19-23

Things to do

Aim: To know the Pentecost story.

Using red, orange and yellow crepe paper, cut strips and bunch some of these strips together to make cheerleader streamers, like this:

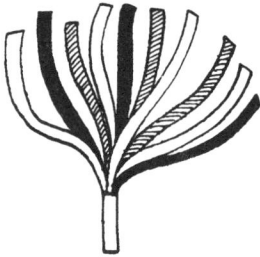

First practise making a collective sound of wind, not by blowing, but breathing out with mouths open. Try it quietly at first, and then much more loudly. We are going to hear about the day when God breathed his life and power into his people.

First tell the children how the disciples were gathered as usual to pray. Just over a week ago they had seen Jesus taken up into heaven, and had been told to wait in Jerusalem for the coming of the Holy Spirit. They had no idea what that meant, or what to expect, but Jesus had told them to wait expectantly.

Now play some quiet music (*Waiting for your Spirit* springs to mind). Suggest we all sit as those disciples did that morning, waiting for God to give us the gift of his Spirit.

Suddenly there was a sound, like this (all start the quiet out-breathing), rather like wind, coming from the sky and getting closer. It was the sound of God, breathing his Holy Spirit into his loyal friends. The sound got louder (all breathe out more loudly), until the whole house they were in seemed surrounded by the living, moving presence of almighty God. (Everyone picks up their streamers and shakers, stands up and whirls them round about as you tell the next part of the story.) Now it was as if tongues of flame flickered out from the breath of God and found each person, resting on them very gently. (The streamers are brought gently down to rest on the floor between the children.)

The disciples were all filled with God's Holy Spirit, and they started praising God and shouting out their love for him. They lifted their hands and all started talking at once. (Put on a praise tape which they know really well, such as *I reach up high*, so they can all dance and sing their hearts out to their God, waving their streamers.)

Still full of God's Spirit, the disciples ran out to share the good news. That's what the Church, including us, has been called to do ever since.

Things to pray

Breathe on me, too, Lord God almighty, as you breathed on the disciples that day.
Touch me with your fire
and set me ablaze with your love!

The Body of Christ

Things to read

Romans 12:3-10
1 Corinthians 12:12-27

Things to do

Aim: To know we are to help one another live in God's way, as members of his team.

Give everyone a building brick (all different sizes and colours) and a drawn plan of the tower they are all going to build. They help one another to get the bricks in the right places, so the tower is completed. They can each only handle their own brick.

Have an outlined person cut from thin card or paper, which is split into chunks as shown below.

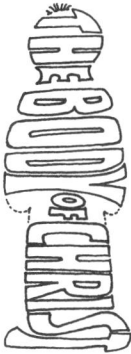

Point out to the children how they all helped one another in the tower building. We all belong to the Church of God, and we have to work together, helping one another so that the church can be what it is meant to be – the Body of Christ (fix the body together so everyone can read it).

What kind of things would we have to do if we were part of the Body of Christ?

Collect all their ideas, which may include such things as going to church, praying, reading the Bible, loving God, helping people, loving people, trying to be good and making mistakes but wanting to put them right. It's true that people should be able to look at Christians and see these things, but most of all they should be able to see that we know we are loved and forgiven by the God who made us. They should be able to see that we know and love the true God.

How can we help one another to be like this? (Get the bricks and build them up as the ideas are mentioned.)

- We can pray together and for one another.
- We can be keen and join in at church so others can see we mean it.
- We can listen and look so we notice if someone is sad or worried.
- We can be a good example by how we behave.

That way we will be working in God's team, as a church, as the Body of Christ, to make the world a better and happier place.

Things to pray

Here I am, Lord.
Help me to live your way
and help me to work with others
so that we can be part of your team.

Spreading the Message

Things to read

Romans 10:13-17
Luke 10:1-11, 16-20

Things to do

Aim: To hear about the mission being sent out by Jesus.

Send people out in pairs with match-boxes, on a mission to collect six different things which fit in their box. Show one another the results when everyone gets back. You can make this a timed activity if your schedule is tight.

First fill in the background to this mission. Jesus began by doing the teaching and healing all over the local area, training his followers or disciples as he went. Jesus realises that there are huge numbers of people all ready to hear the good news, but only a few people to teach them. He talks about it as being like a huge harvest of people, ripe to gather in, but with very few workers to do it. So now he spreads the net wider, by sending out seventy-two of his trained followers. As this is quite a large number to visualise, have seventy-two paper people cut out and spread them all over the floor in the middle of the circle. Let a few children put them into pairs, because Jesus sent these people out in pairs. They can discuss the advantages of this.

Jesus gathered this crowd of people together and gave them their instructions. Have these written out on a large sheet of paper or length of wallpaper:

1. Be careful.
2. Travel light.
3. Don't waste time chatting on the way.
4. 'Peace to this house!'
5. Eat what you are given.
6. Heal the sick in body and mind.
7. Tell them the kingdom of God is very close to them.

Using the cut-out people and a large sheet of paper, make a collage picture of this mission, sticking on the children's drawings of roads, villages, trees and the people hearing the good news everywhere, and being healed.

Things to pray

Lord, so many people
have no idea of how happy they could be
with you at the centre of their life.
Please send us lots more workers
into this harvest,
to let the people know about you
and bring them safely into your
   kingdom. Amen.

Good News for All Nations

Things to read

Genesis 17:1-8
Matthew 28:16-20

Things to do

Aim: To know that the Gospel of Jesus is for all nations.

Tell the children a selection of different greetings, and set them off walking around to music. Whenever the music stops, call out a nationality, and everyone goes round greeting one another appropriately. Here are some suggestions for greetings:

British – shake hands and say, 'How do you do?' 'How do you do?'

Japanese – hands together and bow to each other

American Indian – raise hand and say 'How!' or rub noses

Australian – 'G'day!'

French – kiss both cheeks or say, 'Bonjour!'

Bring along a world map and a selection of books on different life patterns in various countries, with tasters of various foods from around the world. (Many supermarkets have quite a wide selection of breads; other items might be dates, bananas, yams, rice and raw cane sugar.)

You could either introduce these in the circle or have it set up more as a 'market place' with the children walking round looking and sampling while music from other cultures is playing. Then come back and see where some of these places are on the world map. If the map is placed on a table they can be marked with nightlight candles.

Remind the children of how the whole world is God's, and he made it. Use the cut-out sections of the diagram below to explain how God made a promise to Abraham long before Jesus was born: that he would make his family into a chosen nation, and that through this nation the whole world would be blessed. When Jesus came, the second part of that promise started to come true, and it's still coming true now, as more and more of the world hears the good news of God's love.

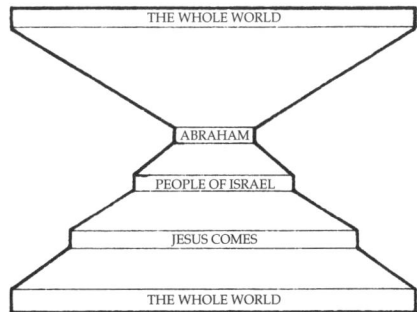

It hasn't been completed yet though. That's why we all pray in the Lord's prayer, 'Let your kingdom come'. There are still people in our world who do not know and need telling. It may well be that some of the children here will spread the Gospel, so that eventually everyone will know.

Things to pray

God, bless our world.
Help us to look after it
and to look after one another.
Let your kingdom come in our world
and let your will be done,
so it is filled with peace and love.
Amen.

Guided by God's Spirit

Things to read

Acts 16:6-10
John 14:15-29

Things to do

Aim: To look at God's provision for us in the leading and guidance of the Holy Spirit.

Pair the children up and blindfold one of the pair. They take it in turns to lead the blindfolded one around the room or grounds, taking great care to protect each other from danger.

Talk over how it felt to be unable to see, and how it helped to have a friend to help us travel safely. When Jesus was with his friends at the last supper he talked to them about having to leave them. They were very sad and rather anxious at the thought of living without their good and wise friend there in person. Jesus had always been able to sort out their fears, cheer them up, get them to make up after arguments, and point out the right things to do. How on earth would they be able to cope without him? And how would they be brave enough to tell other people about him when they knew that would put them in danger?

Read the Gospel passage, asking them to listen out for a promise Jesus gave. They can put their hands up when they hear it, and John 14:16 can be displayed for everyone to read together. So the disciples (and that includes us) were not going to be left like orphans to manage on their own. Somehow God would be with them, in a real and personal way, even though it wouldn't be a person they could see physically.

To get just one idea of how this worked out, tell the children about a time after the Resurrection, when Paul and his friends were travelling round telling people about the God of love. Tell them how the Spirit stopped them going to some places they planned, and led them straight to another place, where some people were ready to hear the good news and become Christians. They can read about it in Acts 16. All over the world, and in each century, God the Holy Spirit is there, guiding people to understand God's will and open doors and nudge in the right direction.

If there is time the children can colour some flags of different countries with the words 'God loves you' written in the appropriate language.

Here are some languages to start you off:

French: Dieu vous aime
German: Gott liebt dich
Italian: Dio ti ama
Spanish: Dios te ama
Swahili: Mungu anakupenda

Things to pray

You could sing *Waiting for your Spirit* and have this prayer during the music interlude between verses:

Lord, I want to go wherever you need me.
Train me to notice
your quiet voice
showing me
the right way to live. Amen.

MISCELLANEOUS

God's Creation

Things to read

Genesis 1:1-2:3
Matthew 6:25-34

Things to do

Aim: To see God's love in his creation.

Use modelling clay to make something they are glad God has made. These can all be gathered on to a tray covered in green and blue paper.

Prepare cut-outs of each creation day's work, which can be stuck on to a blank sheet of paper in order while the Genesis passage is being read. Use these ideas or design your own.

1. A plain sheet of black paper.
2. Sky blue paper to cover half of the top of the black paper. (You'll need to keep some of the 'sky' black.)
3. Shiny blue paper across the bottom part.
4. Brown land shape in the blue sea. Trees with fruit, flowers and grass.
5. Sun in the blue half of sky, moon and stars in the black side.
6. Birds and fish.
7. Animals and humans.
8. The title: 'God saw that it was very good.'

Have some music playing as a background, someone to read the creation story, and someone else to get on with the developing picture, so the narrative is not interrupted but interpreted as it goes along, and the children experience with several senses at once.

Our creative, loving God has given us all this. Isn't it beautiful! If God takes all this care over everything he makes, then we can be sure he will take great care of us, too. We don't need to waste our time worrying and being anxious, because our God is the powerful creative God who brought our whole universe into being and our planet into life.

Things to pray

Throw a ball which is designed to look like the earth, as you sing:

You've got the whole world in your hand,

you've got the whole wide world in your hand,

you've got the whole world in your hand,

you've got the whole world in your hand.

The Holy Trinity

Things to read

2 Corinthians 13:11-13
John 16:12-15

Things to do

Aim: To understand more about the nature of God.

Set out different colours of paints and help them to do colour sums, like this:

Red + Yellow =

Yellow + Blue =

Red + Green =

Beforehand prepare the word 'Trinity' on two pieces of card, with 'Tri' on one piece and 'Unity' on the other.

First look together at the colour sums, and point out the way that although we put clear yellow and clear blue in, you can't see them any more once they've turned green. They have become something different.

Today is called Trinity Sunday, and we're going to look at what that means. Show the cards as 'Trinity'. Then put the 'Unity' bit down and concentrate on the 'Tri'. Talk about words they know which have this in them, such as tricycle, tripod and triangle. Between you work out from these words what 'Tri' means. What has three got to do with God? Draw three dots on a sheet of paper and name them with their help, God the Father, God the Son and God the Holy Spirit.

Now pick up the 'Unity' section. Block off the 'y' and ask what words they know with 'unit' in them, such as united, unit, and unite. If anyone can count in French you can ask them what 'un' means in French. Work out together the meaning of 'Unity'. What has this got to do with God? Draw lines joining the three dots together to form a triangle and explain that there is only one God. But unlike the colours we made, we can still see the three different 'colours' of God in his nature. That's why the Church has squashed the two words 'Tri' and 'Unity' together, to make a word that tries to understand God better. Fix the two pieces of card together again, and put the word next to the drawing.

Things to pray

Glory be to God the Father,
Glory be to God the Son,
Glory be to God the Spirit,
Holy Trinity, three in one!

A Holy Day

Things to read

Isaiah 58:13-14
Luke 13:10-17

Things to do

Aim: To know the story of the crippled woman being healed on the Sabbath.

Use a beanbag or soft ball and make a circle with one person in the centre. They throw the beanbag to each person in turn and have it thrown back to them. After six throws they change with the person they would have thrown to next. Everyone shouts in time to the throwing: 'One, Sunday; two, Monday; three, Tuesday; four, Wednesday; five, Thursday; six, Friday; seven, Saturday, the Sabbath, all change!'

Remind the children of the fourth Commandment – to keep the Sabbath, or seventh day of the week, special and holy, and rest on that day, because it was on the seventh day that God rested from his work of creation.

See if they have any ideas about why we now keep the first day of the week special and holy, instead of the seventh, and tell them how the Jewish religion still celebrates Saturday, the Sabbath. What would they think it meant not to work on the Sabbath? What kind of work would people still have to do? Jot the ideas down in two columns – headed with a tick and a cross. Amongst the obvious 'work' tasks suggest things like preparing food, leading your animals to have a drink, putting out a fire, and rescuing your donkey if it fell into a ditch, so the children can discuss them and decide whether they should be counted as work or not.

Now that they have a taste of the way the Jewish leaders had tried to sort out what the Commandment meant, and can see that if you get too picky you lose sight of what it's really about, tell the story of what happened on one Sabbath day when Jesus was worshipping at the local synagogue. Involve the children in acting it out as you tell the story, and have another leader getting annoyed by the healing and telling everyone not to come for healing on the Sabbath.

Freeze the story there and ask the children what they think. Was this leader right? Was it wrong to heal on the Sabbath? Or was the Sabbath a good day to heal on? After they've said their thoughts, one by one, without comment from you (except encouraging acknowledgement), carry on with the story, and tell them how Jesus reacted to the leader's attitude.

Things to pray

Thank you, Lord God,
for showing us how to be free.
Teach us to notice the needs
of those around us
and make us ready to help. Amen.

Index of Uses

TOPICS

Anointed	24
Ascension	33
Baptism	12, 51
Body	83
Bread	28, 29, 48
Bridesmaids	39
Busy	76
Change	23, 32, 73
Childhood	11
Choosing	52, 58
Christmas	8, 9, 34
Church	82-86
Coin	43, 65
Commandments	58, 63, 73, 90
Communion	48
Co-operation	83
Cost	38, 50, 61
Creation	19, 34, 88
Cross	26, 33, 53, 64
Donkey	25
Easter	27, 33
Egypt	10
Emmaus	28, 29
Enemies	60
Epiphany	9, 15
Escape	10
Faces	60
Faith	20, 30, 31, 33, 49, 51, 67
Faithfulness	56
Fasting	14
First	61
Fishing	16, 32
Foolish	39, 41, 50
Forgiveness	12, 44, 45, 60, 71, 74, 79
Found	43

Free	64
Friend	55
Fruit	63
Generous	59
Growing	37
Guidance	48, 86
Happiness	64, 80
Harvest	17, 84
Healing	18, 90
Heaven	33, 68
Holy Spirit	33, 66, 82, 86
Hospitality	61
Ignore	46
Journey	9, 10, 28, 29, 49, 67, 68
King	9, 25, 26
Kingdom of God	17, 25, 38, 79
Law	58, 63, 73
Light	36, 39
Listening	10, 14, 76
Load	54
Lord's Prayer, The	79
Lost	43
Love	24, 32, 51, 53, 55, 59, 60, 62, 63, 73
Message	17, 74, 84, 85
Miracle	15, 16, 18, 19, 20, 21, 90
Mission	17, 84, 85
Mistakes	23
Mountain	22
Names	59
Nations	85
Need	80
Obedience	8, 42, 51, 52, 53, 62, 64
Others	61
Palm Sunday	25
Parables	36-46, 50, 52, 77, 78
Party	61
Pearl	38

Pentecost 82
Perfume 24
Perseverance 56, 77
Plumb line 73
Poverty 46, 66
Prayer 14, 22, 26, 54, 76-80
Presents 59
Push 61
Questions 9, 21, 30, 31, 64, 65, 68
Ready 12, 39, 74
Repent 12, 74
Resurrection 27, 28, 29, 30, 31, 32
Rush 76
Sabbath 90
Salt 36
Sea 16, 19, 20, 32
Second coming 39
Seed 17, 37
Seeing 30, 31, 33, 86
Seeking 9, 13
Service 56
Sheep 43, 48
Shepherd 48
Sign 9, 15
Sin 12, 64, 74
Slave 64
Soldiers 51
Sorry 23, 32, 71
Sower 37
Star 9
Starting again 23, 32
Storm 19, 20
Suffering 53, 66
Talents 40
Taste 15
Team 8, 17
Temptation 14, 49
Thanks 18
Thirst 66
Touch 30, 31
Transfiguration 22

Trinity 89
Waiting 39, 74
Wants 80
Water 12, 15, 19, 20, 63
Way 49, 58
Wealth 38, 41, 46, 65
Wedding 15, 39
Wine 15
Wise 9, 39
Word 19, 34, 37, 72
Words 52, 62
Yoke 54

BIBLE CHARACTERS

Abraham 67
Amos 73
Andrew 13
Disciples, The 13, 16, 17, 19, 20, 22, 28, 29, 30, 31, 32, 33
Elijah 70, 71
Elizabeth 8
Herod 9, 10
Isaiah 66, 72
James 22
Jesus 8-34, 48-56, 65, 72, 78, 79, 84, 85, 86
Jezebel 71
John 22
John the Baptist 8, 12, 13, 74
Judas 24
Lazarus 24, 46
Lepers, The ten 18
Martha 24, 76
Mary (mother of Jesus) 8
Mary (friend of Jesus) 24, 76
Naboth 71
Nathaniel 13
Paul 86
Peter 13, 16, 20, 21, 22, 27, 32, 55
Pharisees 62, 65

Philip   13
Thomas   30, 31, 49
Wise Men, The   9
Zacchaeus   23

ACTIVITIES

Acted stories   9, 10, 12, 15, 16, 18, 19, 20,
            24, 25, 27, 28, 29, 37, 38, 41, 44, 45,
        46, 50, 56, 61, 68, 70, 71, 76, 77, 78, 82, 90
Action prayers   15, 16, 18, 27, 28,
                    29, 51, 53, 56, 66, 74, 79
Action song   42
Brainstorming   9, 26, 36
Building   50, 83
Buying games   50, 65
Carpet tile pictures   13, 59
Chalk pictures   23
Choosing games   52, 58
Clay modelling   88
Collage   84
Collecting games   17, 38
Colouring   27
Colour mixing   89
Dance   8
Feeding jelly   61
Feeling game   30, 31
Fitness exercises   56, 68
Following instructions   16, 19, 28, 29,
                    42, 51, 53, 62, 63, 64
Follow my leader   53, 67
Greetings game   85
Guessing games   9, 21, 26, 71, 80
I am the music man   40
Imagining   68
Listening games   10, 34, 76
Lion hunt   32
Looking at seeds   37
Measuring   73
Memorising   17, 48, 58, 60

Music 8, 37, 40, 42, 44, 46, 51, 67, 68, 73, 86, 88
My aunt went to Paris   41
News time   34
Newspapers   49
Observation   46
Obstacle course   36
Pairs   13, 14, 61, 84, 86
Passing round circle games   11, 16, 22, 34,
                                  41, 55, 59
Picture making   48
Planting seeds   37
Procession   25
Posters   27, 74
Questions   9, 14, 21, 26, 80
Road map game   28
Scissors, stone, paper   58
Sharings thoughts and ideas   11, 34, 40, 55,
                                  56, 60, 83
Searching games   13, 27, 43, 77, 79, 84
Simon says   19
Smelling game   24
Sorting games   33, 80
Stuck in the mud   71
Tail on a donkey   78
Tasting   15
Team games   8, 42, 60
Testing heartbeat   44
Three-legged race   54
Throwing game   90
Time challenge games   17, 38, 70, 84
Time lines   11, 72
Walk   28, 29
Walkway game   49
Water play   20
What I really need is . . .   66
Word puzzle   72
Visual aids   9, 11, 13, 14, 22, 24, 32, 33,
            38, 42, 43, 48, 54, 58, 63, 64, 65, 66, 67,
                        74, 77, 80, 84, 85, 89
Yes, your majesty   64

BIBLE REFERENCES

Genesis 1:1-3	34
Genesis 1:1-2:3	88
Genesis 2:15-17; 3:1-7	14
Genesis 12:1-4a	67
Genesis 17:1-8	85
Genesis 32:22-31	77
Exodus 14:10-22	20
Exodus 34:29-35	22
Leviticus 19:1-2, 9-18	59
Deuteronomy 30:15-20	58
1 Samuel 2:18-20, 26	11
1 Kings 18:20-39	70
1 Kings 21:1-21a	71
2 Kings 5:1-19	18
Psalm 1	63
Psalm 5:1-8	71
Psalm 23	48
Psalm 31:1-8	10
Psalm 32:1-7	23
Psalm 36:5-10	15
Psalm 65	78
Psalm 65:9-13	37
Psalm 103:8-13	44
Psalm 107:23-32	19
Psalm 112:1-10	36
Psalm 118:1-2, 19-29	25
Psalm 131	76
Psalm 145:8-14	54
Isaiah 9:1-7	72
Isaiah 35	49
Isaiah 42:1-9	12
Isaiah 49:1-7	13
Isaiah 55:1-3a	80
Isaiah 55:1-9	66
Isaiah 58:13-14	90
Isaiah 60:1-6	9
Ezekiel 34:1-6, 11-16	43
Amos 5:14-15, 21-24	62
Amos 7:7-9	73
Malachi 3:1-4	74
Matthew 2:1-12	9
Matthew 2:13-23	10
Matthew 3:13-17	12
Matthew 4:1-11	14
Matthew 4:12-17, 23-25	72
Matthew 5:13-20	36
Matthew 5:17-20	58
Matthew 5:38-48	59
Matthew 6:5-15	79
Matthew 6:25-34	88
Matthew 7:21-29	42
Matthew 9:9-13	62
Matthew 9:35-10:11	17
Matthew 11:25-30	54
Matthew 13:1-9, 18-23	37
Matthew 13:45-46	38
Matthew 14:22-23	20
Matthew 16:13-20	21
Matthew 16:21-25	53
Matthew 18:21-35	44
Matthew 21:1-11	25
Matthew 21:28-31	52
Matthew 22:15-22	65
Matthew 22:34-40	63
Matthew 25:1-13	39
Matthew 25:14-30	40
Matthew 28:16-20	85
Luke 1:26-56	8
Luke 2:41-52	11
Luke 3:1-6	74
Luke 5:1-11	16
Luke 6:27-36	60
Luke 8:22-25	19
Luke 9:28-36	22
Luke 10:1-11, 16-20	84
Luke 10:38-42	76
Luke 12:13-21	41
Luke 13:10-17	90
Luke 14:1, 7-14	61
Luke 14:25-33	50

Luke 15:1-10	43	Acts 4:23-31	79
Luke 16:19-31	46	Acts 11:1-18	55
Luke 17:5-10	56	Acts 13:1-3	17
Luke 17:11-19	18	Acts 16:6-10	86
Luke 18:1-8	77	Romans 6:12-23	64
Luke 18:9-14	78	Romans 10:13-17	84
Luke 19:1-10	23	Romans 12:3-10	83
Luke 20:27-38	68	Romans 12:14-21	60
Luke 23:33-43	26	Romans 13:1-8	65
Luke 24:13-35	28	1 Corinthians 12:12-27	83
Luke 24:44-53	33	1 Corinthians 15:35-44, 49	68
John 1:1-3	34	2 Corinthians 13:11-13	89
John 1:35-51	13	2 Corinthians 2:14-17	24
John 2:1-11	15	Philippians 2:3-7a	61
John 4:5-15	66	Philippians 2:5-11	26
John 6:2-14, 25-35	80	Philippians 3:7-11	38
John 8:31-36	64	Colossians 1:15-20	21
John 10:1-10	48	1 Thessalonians 5:1-11	39
John 12:1-8	24	2 Thessalonians 3:6-15	40
John 14:1-14	49	1 Timothy 6:1-10	41
John 14:15-21	51	1 Timothy 4:6-16	56
John 14:15-29	86	2 Timothy 2:1-5	51
John 15:10-17	55	Hebrews 10:5-10	8
John 16:12-15	89	Hebrews 11:8-10	67
John 20:1-18	27	Hebrews 12:1-3	50
John 20:19-23	82	James 1:22-27	42
John 20:19-31	30	James 2:1-13	73
John 21:1-19	32	James 2:14-18	52
Acts 1:6-14	33	James 5:13-20	70
Acts 2:1-21	82	1 Peter 1:3-9	27
Acts 2:14a, 29-32	28	1 Peter 5:1-4	32
Acts 2:37-42	16	2 Peter 4:12-16	53
Acts 3:1-10	46	1 John 1:1-4	30